RAISING CHILDREN
GOD'S WAY

GW00672412

RAISING CHILDREN
GOD'S WAY

D. Martyn Lloyd-Jones

THE BANNER OF TRUTH TRUST

THE BANNER OF TRUTH TRUST
3 Murrayfield Road, Edinburgh EH12 6EL, UK
P.O. Box 621, Carlisle, PA 17013, USA

First published 1973 in *Life in the Spirit,*
Volume 6 of the Ephesians Series by
D. M. Lloyd-Jones

First published in this form 2007
Reprinted 2011

ISBN: 978 0 85151 958 6

Typeset in 11/14 pt Sabon at
the Banner of Truth Trust

Printed in the USA by
Versa Press, Inc.,
East Peoria, IL

Contents

Publisher's Introduction

The five sermons in this small volume were originally preached in Westminster Chapel on Sunday mornings as part of a lengthy series of expositions of Ephesians and have already appeared in print.[1] The way in which Dr Lloyd-Jones, following the apostle Paul, deals with the relationships of family life is extremely important. He insists that these practical matters cannot be rightly understood apart from the profound truths of the Christian faith to which Paul relates them. To attempt to deal with Christian practice in isolation from Christian doctrine is to tread a dangerous path. In Dr Lloyd-Jones' view, the only Christianity powerful enough to penetrate and change society is that which is derived from the work of the Spirit of God.

In an age which has seen an almost total collapse of family life, when, in many places, most children are being brought up in 'broken homes', Christian families can present a powerful

---

[1] The complete series is published by the Trust in eight volumes. The sermons in this book are taken from the sixth volume, *Life in the Spirit* (*Eph.* 5:18–6:9), ISBN 0 85151 194 5, 372 pp., clothbound.

witness to the supernatural realities which have entered the life of the world through the gospel of Christ. In this way they can point beyond merely practical matters to the profoundest truths of human existence.

The present situation, then, may be seen as giving Christians, and especially Christian families, a valuable opportunity to bear witness to the truth of the gospel. These sermons will afford considerable help in grasping this opportunity.

THE PUBLISHER
April 2007

Raising Children God's Way

Children, obey your parents in the Lord: for this is right. ² Honour thy father and mother; which is the first commandment with promise; ³ That it may be well with thee, and thou mayest live long on the earth. ⁴ And ye fathers, provoke not your children to wrath: but bring them up in the nurture and admonition of the Lord.

EPHESIANS 6:1–4

1. Submissive Children

W E COME, IN EPHESIANS 6:1–4, not only to the beginning of a new chapter in Paul's Epistle to the Ephesians, but also to a new subsection, and a new subject – the relationship of children and parents. As we do so, it is very important for us to bear in mind that this is only a further illustration of the great principle which the Apostle has laid down in the previous chapter,[1] and which he works out in terms of our varied human relationships.

That principle is stated in the eighteenth verse of the fifth chapter, 'And be not drunk with wine, wherein is excess; but be filled with the Spirit.' That is the key, and all he says from there on is but an illustration of how the life of a Christian man or woman, who is filled with the Spirit, is lived in various respects. Another subsidiary general principle was stated in the twenty-first verse, 'Submitting yourselves one to another in the fear of God.'

In other words we have to bear in mind that the Apostle is contending that the Christian life is an entirely new life,

[1] This and the following chapters were originally part of a series of expository sermons on the Epistle to the Ephesians, preached by D. M. Lloyd-Jones on Sunday mornings at Westminster Chapel, London, between 1954 and 1962. The complete series is published by the Banner of Truth Trust in 8 volumes. The volume from which these sermons are taken is *Life in the Spirit* (5:18–6:9), ISBN 0 85151 194 5, 372 pp., clothbound.

altogether different from the 'natural' life even at its very best. He was primarily concerned to contrast this new life with the old pagan life which these people had been living before their conversion; and it is virtually the difference between a man who is drunk and a man who is filled with the Spirit of God. I remind you of this in order to emphasize that what we have here is not mere ethics or morality; this is the application of Christian doctrine and Christian truth.

Having worked out his principle in terms of husbands and wives the Apostle now proceeds to do the same in terms of the relationships within the family, especially that between parents and children, and children and parents. All will agree that this is a tremendously important subject at this present time. We are living in a world which is witnessing an alarming breakdown in the matter of discipline.

Lawlessness is rampant, there is a breakdown in discipline in all these fundamental units of life – in marriage and in home relationships. A spirit of lawlessness is abroad, and things which were once more or less taken for granted are not only being queried and questioned but are being ridiculed and dismissed. There is no question but that we are living in an age when there is a ferment of evil working actively in the whole of society.

We can go further, and I am simply saying something that all observers of life are agreed about, whether they are Christians or not, and say that in many ways we are face to face with a total collapse and breakdown of what is called 'civilization' and society. And there is no respect in which this is more evident and obvious than in this matter of the relationship of parents and children.

I know that much of what we are witnessing is probably a reaction from something that was far too common, unfortunately, at the end of the Victorian era and in the early years of this present century. I shall have more to say about that later, but I mention it now in passing in order to set out this problem clearly. There is, no doubt, a reaction against the stern, legalistic and almost cruel Victorian type of father. I am not excusing the present position, but it is important that we should understand it and try to trace its origin. But whatever the cause there is no doubt that it is part and parcel of this collapse in the whole matter of discipline and law and order.

The Bible in its teaching and in its history tells us that this is something that always happens at a time of irreligion, at a time of godlessness. For instance we have a notable example in what the Apostle Paul says about the world in the Epistle to the Romans in the second half of the first chapter, from verse 18 to the end. There he gives an appalling description of the state of the world at the time when our Lord came into it. It was a state of sheer lawlessness. And in the various manifestations of that lawlessness which he lists, he includes this very matter we are now considering. First he says, 'God gave them over to a reprobate mind, to do those things which are not convenient' (verse 28). Then follows the description: 'Being filled with all unrighteousness, fornication, wickedness, covetousness, maliciousness; full of envy, murder, debate, deceit, malignity; whisperers, backbiters, haters of God, despiteful, proud, boasters, inventors of evil things, disobedient to parents, without understanding, covenant-breakers, without natural affection, implacable, unmerciful . . .' In that horrible list Paul includes this idea of being disobedient to parents.

Again, in the second Epistle to Timothy, probably the last letter he ever wrote, we find him saying in the third chapter, verse 2: 'In the last days perilous times shall come.' Then he states the characteristics of such times: 'For men shall be lovers of their own selves, covetous, boasters, proud, blasphemers, disobedient to parents, unthankful, unholy, without natural affection' – that has gone – 'trucebreakers, false accusers, incontinent, fierce, despisers of those that are good, traitors, heady, high-minded, lovers of pleasures more than lovers of God.'

In both instances the Apostle reminds us that at a time of apostasy, at a time of gross godlessness and irreligion, when the very foundations are shaking, one of the most striking manifestations of the lawlessness is 'disobedience to parents'. So it is not at all surprising that he should call attention to it here, as he gives us illustrations of how the life that is 'filled with the Spirit' of God manifests itself.

When will the civil authorities learn and realize that there is an indissoluble connection between godlessness and a lack of morality and decent behaviour? There is an order in these matters. 'The wrath of God is revealed from heaven', says the Apostle in Romans 1:18, 'against all ungodliness and unrighteousness of men.' If you have ungodliness you will always have unrighteousness.

But the tragedy is that the civil authorities, irrespective of which political party is in power, all seem to be governed by modern psychology rather than by the Scriptures. They all are convinced that they can deal with unrighteousness directly, in and by itself. But that is impossible. Unrighteousness is always the result of ungodliness; and the only hope of getting back any measure of righteousness into life is to have a revival of godliness. That is precisely what the Apostle is saying to the Ephesians and to ourselves. The best and the most moral periods in the history of this country, and every other country, have always been those periods which have followed mighty religious awakenings. This problem of lawlessness and lack of discipline, the problem of children and of youth, was just not present fifty years ago as it is today. Why? Because the great tradition of the Evangelical Awakening of the eighteenth century was still operating. But as that has gone, these terrible moral and social problems are coming back, as the Apostle teaches us, and as they have always come back throughout the running centuries.

Present conditions therefore demand that we should look at the Apostle's statement. I believe that Christian parents and children, Christian families, have a unique opportunity of witnessing to the world at this present time by just being different. We can be true evangelists by showing this discipline, this law and order, this true relationship between parents and children. We may be the means under God's hand of bringing many to a knowledge of the truth. Let us therefore think of it in that way.

But there is a second reason why we all need this teaching, for, according to the Scriptures, it is not only needed by those who are not Christians in the way I have been indicating, but Christian people also need this exhortation, because the devil often comes in at this point in a most subtle manner and tries to sidetrack us. In the fifteenth chapter of Matthew's Gospel our Lord takes up this point with the religious people of his day, because they were, in a very subtle way, evading one of the plain injunctions of the Ten Commandments. The Ten Commandments told them to honour their parents, to respect them and to care for them; but what was happening was that some of those people, who claimed to be ultra-religious, instead of doing what the Commandment told them to do, said in effect, 'Ah, I have dedicated this money which I have to the Lord; I therefore cannot look after you, my parents.' This is how he puts it: 'Ye say, Whosoever shall say to his father or mother, It is a gift, by whatsoever thou mightest be profited by me; and honour not his father or his mother, he shall be free.' They were saying, 'This is Corban, this is dedicated to the Lord. Of course I would like to look after you and help you, and so on, but this has been dedicated to the Lord.' In this way they were neglecting their parents and their duties towards them.

That was a very subtle danger, and it is a danger that is still present with us. There are young people who are doing great harm to the Christian cause today through being deluded by Satan at this very point. They are being rude to their parents, and what is still more serious, they are rude to their parents in

terms of their Christian ideas and their Christian service. Thus
they are a stumbling-block to their own unconverted parents.
Such Christians cannot see that we do not put these great
Commandments on one side when we become Christians, but
that, rather, we should live them out and exemplify them more
than we have ever done before.

Let us then, in the light of these things, notice how the
Apostle states the matter. He starts, using the same principle as
he used in the case of the married relationship, with the
children. That is to say, he starts with those who are under
obedience, those who are to be subject. He started with the
wives, and then went on to the husbands. Here he starts with
the children and then goes on to the parents. He does so
because he is illustrating this fundamental point, 'Submitting
yourselves one to another in the fear of the Lord.' The
injunction is, 'Children, obey your parents.' And then he
reminds them of the Commandment, 'Honour thy father and
mother.'

In passing we note the interesting point that here, once
again, we have something that differentiates Christianity from
paganism. The pagans, in these matters did not link the mother
with the father, but spoke of the father only. But the Christian
position, as indeed the Jewish position, as given by God to
Moses, puts the mother with the father. The injunction is that
children are to obey their parents, and the word 'obey' means
not only to listen to, but to listen as realizing that you are
under authority, to listen 'under'. You are looking up for a
commandment, and you not only listen, but you recognize
your position of subservience, and you proceed to put it into
practice.

But it is most important that this should be governed and
controlled by the accompanying idea, that of 'honouring'.
'Honour thy father and mother.' That means 'respect',
'reverence'. This is an essential part of the Commandment.
Children are not to give a mechanical and a grudging

obedience. That is quite wrong; that is to observe the letter but not the spirit. That is what our Lord condemned so strongly in the Pharisees. No, they are to observe the spirit as well as the letter of the law. Children are to reverence and to respect their parents. They are to realize the position which obtains between them, and they are to rejoice in it. They are to regard it as a great privilege, and therefore they must go out of their way always to show this reverence and respect in their every action.

The Apostle's appeal implies that Christian children should be entirely different from godless children, who generally show lack of reverence for parents and ask, 'Who are they?', 'Why should I listen?' They regard their parents as 'back numbers' and speak of them disrespectfully. They assert themselves and their own rights and their 'modernism' in this whole matter of conduct.

That was happening in the pagan society out of which these Ephesians had come, as it is happening in the pagan society that is round and about us at this present time.

We read constantly in the newspapers of how this lawlessness is coming in, and how children, so it is worded, 'are maturing at an earlier age'. There is no such thing, of course. Physiology does not change. What is changing is the mentality and the outlook leading to aggressiveness, and a failure to be governed by biblical principles and biblical teaching. One hears of this on all hands: young people speaking disrespectfully to their parents, looking disrespectfully at them, flouting everything that they tell them, and asserting themselves and their own rights.

It is one of the most ugly manifestations of the sinfulness and the lawlessness of this present age. Now, over and against all such behaviour, the Apostle says, 'Children, obey your parents; honour your father and mother, treat them with respect and reverence, show that you realize your position and what it means.'

But let us look at the Apostle's reasons for giving the injunction. The first is, and I am taking them in this particular order for a reason which will emerge later, 'For this is right.' By this he means: It is righteous, it is something which is essentially right and good in and of itself. Are you surprised that the Apostle puts it like that? There are certain Christian people – they generally claim for themselves an unusual degree of spirituality – who always object to this kind of reasoning. They say, 'I no longer think along the natural level; I am a Christian now.'

But the great Apostle did not speak in that way. He says, 'Children, obey your parents.' 'Why should I obey my parents?', says someone. My first answer is, 'It is right'; this is a righteous thing to do. The Christian does not despise that level; he starts with the natural level.

What Paul means by 'right', in other words, is this: he is going back to the whole order of creation laid down at the very beginning, away back in the book of Genesis. We have already seen that in dealing with husbands and wives he did exactly the same thing; he went back and he quoted from the second chapter of Genesis: 'For this cause shall a man leave his father and mother and shall be joined unto his wife, and they two shall be one flesh.' He did not hesitate, in dealing with the married relationship, to say in effect, 'I am only asking you to do what is foundational, what is natural, what has obtained from the very beginning as regards man and woman, husband and wife.'

And now, he tells us that, with regard to this question of children, the principle is there at the beginning; it has always been so, it is a part of the order of nature, it is a part of the basic rule of life. This is something you find not only among human beings, it operates even among the animals. In the animal world, the mother cares for the young offspring that has just been born, looks after it, feeds it, protects it. Not only that, she teaches it how to do various things. She teaches a little bird how to use its wings, a little animal how to walk and to stumble and to struggle along. This is the order of nature. The young creature in its weakness and ignorance needs the protection and the guidance and the help and the instruction which is given by the parent. So, says the Apostle, 'Obey your parents . . . for this is right.' Christians are not divorced from a natural order found everywhere in creation.

It is a regrettable thing that this needs to be said to Christians at all. How does it become possible that people can deviate at any point from something that is so patently obvious and belongs to the very order and course of nature? Even the wisdom of the world recognizes this. There are people around us who are not Christians at all but they are firm believers in discipline and order.

Why? Because the whole of life and the whole of nature indicates this. For an offspring to be rebellious against the parents and to refuse to listen and to obey is something ridiculous and foolish. We see animals doing it sometimes and we are amused at them. But how much more ridiculous it is when that kind of thing is done by a human being! It is unnatural for children not to obey their parents; they are violating something that is clearly a part of the whole warp and woof of human nature, seen everywhere, from top to bottom. Life has been planned on this basis. And if it were not, of course, life would soon become chaotic, and it would end its own existence.

'This is right!' There is something about this aspect of the teaching of the New Testament which seems to me to be very wonderful. It shows that you must not divide the Old Testament from the New Testament. There is nothing which displays more ignorance than for a Christian to say, 'Of course, being a Christian now, I am not interested in the Old Testament.' That is entirely wrong because, as the Apostle reminds us here, it is the God who created at the beginning who is the God who saves. It is one God from beginning to end. God made male and female, parents and children, right through the whole of nature. He did it in that way, and life is to work along these principles. So the Apostle starts his exhortation by virtually saying: 'This is right, this is basic, this is fundamental, this is part of the order of nature. Do not go back on that; if you do you are denying your Christianity, you are denying the God who established life after this fashion and made it work according to these principles. Obedience is right.'

But having spoken thus the Apostle proceeds to his second point. This is not only right, he says, this is also 'the first commandment with promise'. 'Honour thy father and thy mother; which is the first commandment with promise.' He means that the honouring of parents is not only essentially right, but that it is actually one of the things that God pinpointed in the Ten Commandments. This is the fifth commandment, 'Honour thy father and thy mother.'

Here again is an interesting point. In a sense there was nothing new in the Ten Commandments. Why then were they ever given? For this reason, that mankind, the children of Israel included, in its sin and its folly had forgotten and strayed away from these fundamental laws of God pertaining to the whole of life. So God, as it were, said, 'I am going to state them again one by one; I am going to write them and underline them so that people shall see them clearly.' It had always been wrong to be disobedient to parents; it had always been wrong to steal and to commit adultery. Those laws did not start at the giving of the Ten Commandments. What the Ten Commandments were designed to do was to impress them upon the minds of people, to state them clearly and to say, 'These are the things you must observe.' The first commandment with promise, the fifth commandment in the Decalogue! God has gone out of his way to call attention to this very thing.

What does the Apostle mean by the expression 'first commandment with promise?' This is a difficult point and we cannot be quite final in our answer. It obviously does not mean that this is the first commandment which has a promise attached to it, for it will be noticed that none of the other commandments have a promise attached to them at all. If it were true to say that commandments six, seven, eight, nine, and ten had promises attached to them, then it could be said, 'Paul means of course that this is the "first" of the commandments to which he attaches a promise.' But there is not a promise attached to the others, so it cannot bear that meaning.

What then does it mean? It may mean that here in this fifth commandment we begin to have instruction with respect to our relationships to one another. Until then it has been our relationship to God, his name, his day, and so on. But here he turns to our relationships with one another; so it may be the first in that sense. Over and above that, however, it may mean that it is the first commandment, not so much in order as in rank, that God was anxious to impress this upon the minds of the children of Israel to such an extent that he added this promise in order to enforce it. First, as it were, in rank, first in importance! Not that ultimately any one of these is more important than the others, for they are all important. Nevertheless there is a relative importance, and I would there-fore view it like this, that this is one of those laws which, when neglected, leads to the collapse of society.

Whether we like it or not, a breakdown in home-life will eventually lead to a breakdown everywhere. This is, surely, the most menacing and dangerous aspect of the state of society at this present time. Once the family idea, the family unit, the family life is broken up – once that goes, soon you will have no other allegiance. It is the most serious thing of all. And that is perhaps the reason why God attached this promise to it.

But I believe that there is even a further suggestion here. There is something about this relationship of children to parents which is unique in this sense, that it points to a yet higher relationship. After all, God is our Father. That is the term he himself uses; that is the term our Lord uses in his model prayer, 'Our Father, which art in heaven'. The earthly father therefore is, as it were, a reminder of that other Father, the heavenly Father. In the relationship of children to parents we have a picture of the relationship of all mankind originally to God. We are all 'children' face to face with God. He is our Father, 'we are all his offspring' (*Acts* 17:28). So in a very wonderful way the relationship between the parent and the child is a replica and a picture, a portrayal, a preaching of this whole relationship that subsists especially between those who are Christian and God himself.

In the third chapter of this Epistle there is a reference to the matter in the fourteenth and fifteenth verses. The Apostle says, 'For this cause, I bow my knees unto the Father of our Lord Jesus Christ, of whom the whole family in heaven and earth is named.' Some say that the translation here should be, 'God is the Father of all fathers.' Whether that is so or not, there is at any rate this suggestion, that the whole relationship of father and child should always remind us of our relationship to God. In that sense this particular relationship is unique. That is not true of the relationship of husband and wife which, as we have seen, reminds us of Christ and the church. But this relationship reminds us of God himself as Father and ourselves as children. There is something very sacred about the family, about this relationship between parents and children; and God, as it were, has told us so in the Ten Commandments. When he came to lay down this commandment, 'Honour thy father and mother', he attached a promise to it.

What promise? 'That it may be well with thee, and that thou mayest live long on the earth.' There can be no doubt that, as the promise was originally given to the children of Israel, it meant the following: 'If you want to go on living in this land of promise to which I am leading you, observe these commandments, this one in particular. If you want to have a time of blessedness and happiness in that promised land, if you want to go on living there under my blessing, observe these commandments, especially this one.' There is no doubt that that was the original promise.

But now the Apostle generalizes the promise because he is dealing here with Gentiles as well as Jews who had become Christians. So he says in effect, 'Now if you want everything to be well with you, and if you want to live a long and a full life on the earth, honour your father and mother.' Does that mean that, if I am a dutiful son or daughter, I am of necessity going to live to great age? No, that does not follow. But the promise certainly means this, that if you want to live a blessed life, a full life under the benediction of God, observe this commandment. He may choose to keep you for a long time on this earth as an example and illustration. But however old you may be when you leave this world, you will know that you are under the blessing and the good hand of God.

We must not regard these things in a mechanical manner. What it is meant to convey is that God is very well pleased with people who observe this commandment, and that if we set ourselves to observe these commandments, and this one in particular, for the right reason, then God will look down with pleasure upon us, and will smile upon us and bless us. Thank God for such a promise!

That brings us to the third and last point. You notice how the Apostle puts it: 'Children, obey your parents. Honour thy father and mother.' Nature dictates it, but not only nature, the law dictates it. But we must go beyond that: to Grace! This is the order – nature, law, grace. 'Children, obey your parents *in the Lord.*' It is important that we should attach that phrase 'in the Lord' to the right word. It does not mean 'Children, obey your parents in the Lord.' It is, rather, 'Children, obey in the Lord your parents.' In other words, the Apostle is repeating the very thing he said in the case of husbands and wives. 'Wives, submit yourselves unto your own husbands *as unto the Lord*'.

'Husbands, love your wives, *even as Christ also loved the church*.'

When we come to his words about servants we shall find him saying, 'Servants, be obedient to them that are your masters according to the flesh *as unto Christ*.' That is what *in the Lord* means. In other words, this is the supreme reason. We are to obey our parents and honour them and respect them because it is a part of our obedience to our Lord and Saviour Jesus Christ. Ultimately that is why we are to do it. Nature dictates it, law has emphasized it, but as Christians we have this further reason, this great and mighty reason: he asks us to do it; it is his commandment; it is one of the ways in which we show our relationship to him and our obedience to him. 'Children, obey your parents *as unto the Lord*.' There are these subsidiary reasons, but you must not stop at them, but obey the command for Christ's sake.

Here again let me emphasize the point that this is highly typical of the New Testament teaching. Christianity never does away with nature. Do not misunderstand me; I am not saying 'fallen nature'. I am saying 'nature', that which God originally created and ordained. Christianity never contradicts nature in that sense. There were people early in the Christian era who thought that it did so even in the married relationship. Paul had to write the seventh chapter of 1 Corinthians for that reason. Some at Corinth were arguing in this way: 'I have become a Christian, my wife has not done so. Well then, because I am a Christian and she is not, I will leave her.' And wives were saying the same. But that is wrong, says Paul. Christianity never calls upon us to deny or to go against nature; we are never meant to be unnatural. What Christianity does is to lift up and sanctify the natural.

The same is true of the law. Christianity does not do away with the law as a portrayal of life. What it does is to add grace to it, enabling us to carry out the law. 'Children, honour thy father and mother.' The law gave that command, Christianity does the same; but it gives us this greater reason for obeying it, it gives us an insight and an understanding into it. We who are Christians realize that we are doing it 'as unto the Lord', the Lord who came from heaven. He came from heaven to honour his Father's law. He kept the law, he lived according to the law. And he has redeemed us that we might be 'a peculiar people, zealous of good works', that we might 'fulfil' the law. He gave himself for us, 'that the righteousness of the law might be fulfilled in us, who walk not after the flesh, but after the Spirit' (*Rom.* 8:4). Grace raises the commandment to the highest level, and we are to obey our parents, and to honour them, and to respect them in order to please our Lord and Saviour who is looking down upon us. The Apostle has said this already in the third chapter, in verse 10: 'To the intent that now unto the principalities and powers in the heavenly places might be known *by the church* the manifold wisdom of God.' Do you realize that as the angels and principalities and powers look down upon us Christian people, and see us exemplifying these things in our daily lives, they are amazed that he, the Son, has ever been able to make such people of us, that we can live according to the commandments of God in a sinful world such as this?

Do it 'as unto the Lord'. Obey your father and mother 'in the Lord'. That is the finest and greatest inducement of all. It gives him pleasure; it is a proof of what he said; we are substantiating his teaching. He said he had come into the world to redeem us, to wash away our sins, to give us a new nature, to make us new men and women. Well, says the Apostle, prove it, show it in practice. Children, show it by obeying your parents; you will be unlike all other children; you will be unlike those arrogant, aggressive, proud, boastful, evil-speaking children that are round about you at the present time. Show that you are different, show that the Spirit of God is in you, show that you belong to Christ. You have a wonderful opportunity; and it will give him great joy and great pleasure.

But let us go even further. 'Children, obey your parents', for this reason also, that when he was in this world he did so. This is what I find in Luke 2:51: 'And he went down with them, and came to Nazareth, and was subject unto them.' The words refer to the Lord Jesus at the age of twelve. He had been up to Jerusalem with Joseph and Mary. They were making their return journey, and they had travelled for a day before they discovered that he was not in the company. They went back and found him in the Temple reasoning and debating and arguing with the doctors of the law, and confuting and confounding them. They were staggered and amazed. And he said, 'Wist ye not that I must be about my Father's business?' He had this dawning realization at the age of twelve. But then we are told that he went back with them to Nazareth: 'He went down with them, and came to Nazareth, and was subject unto them.' The Son of God incarnate submitting himself to Joseph and Mary! Though he had this consciousness within him that he was in this world, about his Father's business, he humbled himself and was obedient unto his parents. Let us look at him, let us realize that he was doing it primarily to please his Father in heaven, that he might fulfil his law in every respect and leave us an example that we might follow in his steps.

There, then, you have the reasons for this injunction, and surely there is no more to be said. It is right. Nature dictates it. It is established by God's law, underwritten, underlined. It pleases the Lord. Obedience is proof that you are like him, for you are doing what he himself did when he was here in this sinful, evil world. May God enlighten us one by one to the importance of observing this injunction!

We shall see that the Apostle goes on as he always does. He has a balanced teaching, so he has a word to say to parents also. What we have said can be misunderstood. If parents stop at this they are guilty of grievous misunderstanding. Paul has not finished; there is a word for parents still to come. But so far this is the word to the children. And as we read it in the light of what he says to parents, we shall be able, perhaps, to deal with some of the problems confronting certain children, whatever their age, who may have parents who are not Christians, and who are wondering what they should do. May God give us all grace to heed this injunction!

2. Unbelieving Parents

WE HAVE SEEN that this subject of parents and their children, which is always important, is unusually so at this present time. And it is important for all of us. It not only concerns children as such, and young people; and not only parents who have children; this is a subject that belongs and applies to all. There is something rather pathetic in the fact that certain Christian people seem to divorce themselves from these matters. I have heard of some, for instance, who have a feeling that the subject of husbands and wives has nothing to do with them because they are not married. That is most regrettable because, whether married or not, whether parents or not, Christians should be interested in principles of truth. Moreover if you are not married yourself you may have a married friend who may be in trouble about his or her married life; so if you are to function as a Christian you must be able to help such a person. To do so you must know how to help, and you can only discover how to help by understanding the scriptural teaching. No-one should sit back therefore, and feel that this has nothing to do with him or her. You may be unmarried, or you may be married but without children, but you should have sympathy with and compassion for parents at the present time in this difficult modern world. It is your duty and business to help them and to assist them. These particular injunctions are not only for particular people, they are for all of us.

But, over and above that, we should all be interested in the opening out of divine truth and in observing how God in his infinite kindness and wisdom and condescension comes to meet us in our various situations as we travel through this world. The civil authorities themselves recognize the importance of the whole problem at the present time. An important Commission on the whole question of education has stated recently that one of the most urgent problems confronting this country today is the breakdown in home and in family life. We are looking therefore at something on which the whole future of society, and of this country, may well depend. Of all people it is we who are Christians who should be giving urgent attention to these matters in order that we may set an example to others and show them how to live as children and parents, and how family and home life should be conducted.

So far we have been looking at the position only from the standpoint of the children, and the injunction that comes to them is that they are to obey their parents. But now in the fourth verse the Apostle puts before us the other side. 'And ye fathers', he says, 'provoke not your children to wrath.' It is not that this addition neutralizes what the Apostle has been saying about the children; it is given, rather, to safeguard it, and to remove every hindrance that may be in the path of children in giving obedience to their parents. It is another notable illustration of the balance and the fairness of the Scriptures. How can anybody face to face with this perfect balance, this fairness, this putting of the two sides together always, deny that this is the inspired Word of God? We have seen its divine character in the case of husbands and wives, and here we find it again in the case of parents and children; and we shall find it later in the case of masters and servants.

The obedience required of the children must be yielded to every kind of parent. There are parents who are guilty of provoking their children to wrath. Now let us be clear that the Apostle's teaching is that the children are to obey even such parents. It is a general statement. The command is to be obeyed without regard of the character of the parents, and it applies even in the case of non-Christian parents.

I want to examine this aspect of the matter carefully because I can say truthfully out of a long pastoral experience that this is one of the commonest problems I have had to deal with, as people have come and spoken to me about the difficulties in their personal lives. You remember what our Lord said in Matthew 10:34: 'Think not that I am come to send peace on earth: I came not to send peace, but a sword.' He said that his teaching was not going to smooth things over, but rather to create division, dividing father and son, mother and daughter, and so on; the reason being that, when a person becomes a Christian, there is such a profound change that it immediately has its effects in all spheres. And there is no realm where this is felt more acutely than in that of the most intimate and most personal relationships; for the moment a person becomes a Christian he or she realizes that the final allegiance is to God and to the Lord Jesus Christ. That inevitably has its effect upon every other form of allegiance. So our Lord says that he is going to be a cause of division: 'A man's foes shall be those of his own household.' You need to be prepared, he says, for these possibilities; and in actual practice this does prove to be the case.

The problem that arises acutely and frequently is that of children who have become Christians, whose parents have not become Christians. A state of tension arises immediately. What are these children to do? How are they to behave? I am simply emphasizing that the Apostle says that these children, or young people (the term 'children' must not be thought of purely in terms of age) are to obey the commandment. What he is saying is, 'Children, obey your parents whether they are Christians or non-Christians, no matter what they are like.' It is a general statement, and a general injunction; but unfortunately it is a point at which very much unconscious harm is often done by many young Christians. There is, perhaps, more failure just at this point than at any other. How are these children to conduct themselves with regard to their non-Christian parents? That is the problem. Unconsciously such children often do much harm through a failure to understand the biblical teaching at this point, and through a lack of balance in their whole outlook. Often they are the cause of antagonizing their own parents from the Christian faith. It is therefore a most important matter.

There is only one qualification which must be added to this general injunction, 'Children, obey your parents', and that one qualification is where our relationship to God is involved in a vital sense. I weigh my words with particular care at this point. If your parents are trying to prohibit you from worshipping God, and giving him obedience, in that case you do not obey your parents. If they are deliberately inciting you, or trying to compel you, to sin, to acts of sin, again you must refuse. But that is the only qualification.

Short of that (and I emphasize this) we must go to the extreme limit; and even in this matter, where we have to face the question as to whether they are standing between us and our relationship to God, we must again go to the extreme limit of conciliation and of concession.

It is just there, I find in pastoral experience, that most people get into difficulties. I mean that as Christians they take a stand on what I would regard as completely unimportant details. Of course that is very natural. We are all by nature people of extremes; and having become Christians we know exactly how we should live. Our great danger at that point – and the devil undoubtedly comes in – is to stand on utterly ridiculous points which really are quite immaterial, and which do not affect our Christian position at all.

Let me give you an illustration. It often comes up, I find, over the question of a marriage service, or the whole question of marriage. Two Christian young people decide to get married, and the parents in both instances are not Christians. The two young Christians are most anxious that this should be an excellent example of Christian marriage and they intend to invite their Christian friends to it. But, of course, the parents have to be present also, the non-Christian parents on both sides, and also some of their friends and relations who are not Christian. I have found so often that the tendency of these excellent young Christian people is to take a stand on matters of details in the service which do not matter, and thereby do much more harm than good. In other words, they say that everything must be exclusively Christian; and they tend to press that to such a point that it becomes an offence to the non-Christians who are present.

It is just there, I feel, that they fail to exercise the judgment and the balance found in the Scriptures. Of course there has to be a Christian service, but there are many other incidental matters in the arrangements which seem to me to be matters of sheer indifference. If we are to be truly Christian we are to make concessions at that point as much as we can, and do everything possible to make it easy for the others, hoping that when they see what a Christian marriage really is they will be attracted to the faith. But if we take a rigid stand and will not make any concession on any point or detail, and insist that it has to be done in our way, in other words, if we are more concerned about impressing our Christian friends than in helping our unbelieving parents, then we are not fulfilling this apostolic injunction about obeying our parents. That is what I mean by standing only on matters which are really vital, and not merely on unimportant and incidental details.

Furthermore, it is important that when we do take a stand we should do so in the right spirit. If we are standing on some Christian principle we must never do so in a contemptuous or impatient manner. Still less must we ever do so in an arrogant manner, or in a censorious manner. We betray ourselves very often in the way in which we say things. I have noticed that people who are guilty of this failure often reveal their wrong attitude even as they discuss the wedding arrangements with me. They say to me with a smile and a smirk on their faces, 'Of course my parents are not Christians'; and dismiss them like that. The moment a person speaks in that way I know that he or she is already in the wrong. Any stand that such a person may take on Christian grounds is almost certain to be useless, and it is liable to do much more harm than good. If your parents are not Christians you should not speak about them in that way; you must not dismiss them, you must not speak with contempt about them. You should be heart-broken because of them, and therefore you should speak of them with grief, with sorrow. But I find that far too often there is glibness and a hardness that are not Christian.

Such 'children' are not obeying their parents, they are not honouring their father and mother. You have to honour your father and mother whether they are Christians or not; that is the injunction.

It is often difficult, but this is the injunction; and I repeat that there is only one limit, namely, the point at which they try, definitely and deliberately, to prevent your worshipping God and serving him, or try to lead you deliberately into the commission of sin. The spirit in which we act at that point is of vital importance; and whenever we reach the stage at which we really have to stand and disobey, we should do so in such a manner as to give the impression that it grieves us, and hurts us, that we are sorry, and that it is a most dreadful decision. For a child to have to stand against a parent is one of the most solemn and serious things we can ever be called upon to do in this life; so whenever it is done in the name of Christ and of God it should be done with a broken heart. We must not fail to give our parents the impression that it is hurting us and causing us grief and costing us much, that we would cut off our right hand in order to avoid it; but that we have no choice in the matter.

If it is done in that way it may well be used of God to influence them; but if it is done arrogantly, contemptuously and censoriously it will certainly do harm. It will be of no value at all, it will drive people away from Christ, it will make them feel and say, 'These children, since they have become Christians, are opinionated, are know-alls, are hard and rigid and legalistic.' It will set up a terrible barrier between them and their coming to a knowledge of God and of our Lord and Saviour. Any stand we feel compelled to take should always be done with a broken heart, with a spirit that is bowed and humbled. We should give the impression that our very hearts are bleeding as we are compelled by this marvellous thing which God has done to us to have to oppose our parents. We must always think of it in that way.

Let me give some reasons why we should do so in order that we all may be helped and guided whenever we find ourselves in such a position. Why is it that the Christian should behave in the manner I have been indicating, both negatively and positively? The answer is, because the Christian child should be the best type of child in the world. That is a general statement, a universal statement. Whatever the Christian does he should always be doing it at its very best. I lay that down as a general proposition. The Christian child should be a better child than any other child, the Christian husband a better husband, the Christian wife a better wife, the Christian family the best type of family in the whole world, the Christian businessman the best businessman conceivable, the professional man the best man in the profession. I do not mean from the standpoint of ability, but from all other aspects. Everything the Christian does should be done with all his might, and with a thoroughness and with an understanding which nobody else is capable of.

That of course is the background to all these detailed injunctions which we are studying. The Christian, remember, is a man who is filled with the Spirit: 'Be not drunk with wine, wherein is excess, but be filled with the Spirit.' Now when any child is 'filled with the Spirit', by definition that child will be an exemplary child, a better child altogether than one of whom this is not true.

To what, then, does that lead? To the conclusion that Christian children should be the best children in the world because they alone have a real and a true understanding of this relationship. There is a breakdown in family and home life today because both sides, parents and children, do not understand the meaning of these things. They know nothing about the relationship of parents and children from the biblical angle. They cannot see these things 'in the Lord', as we are to see them; but because we are 'in the Lord' we have a new understanding about these things. We see that this relationship of parent and child is a reflection and a picture of the relationship of God and the Christian who is his child. So we have this exalted, elevated notion of parenthood and of the relationship of the children to their parents. It is because the Christian child alone has an understanding of these matters, and of this relationship, that he or she should always excel others in practice. As Christians we do not act automatically. The Christian always knows why he does anything. He has his reasons, he has these explanations and expositions of Scripture; so he understands the situation.

Then it is the Christian alone who has the right spirit: 'Be filled with the Spirit.' The whole problem in these matters is ultimately one of spirit. The modern attitude is, 'Why should I listen to my parents. Who are they? Back numbers, out of date in any case! What do they understand?' That is the spirit that is causing so much trouble today. The parents, on the other hand, are guilty of the same failure in spirit. 'These children are a nuisance', they often say. 'We like to be going out in the evenings as we used to, but the children have arrived and we can no longer do so.' The spirit is already wrong, and that is why there are so many failures. These problems are all matters of 'the spirit', and that is why the pathetic politicians and statesmen, with their Acts of Parliament, are not even beginning to see the nature of the problem with which they are dealing. You cannot legislate about these matters; it is a matter of the spirit.

It is very important that the Christian child should have the right spirit in these matters; and the last thing he must be guilty of is a selfish spirit. I have referred to that earlier. Here is this very delicate position. These Christian young people are about to be married, and there are these non-Christian parents. The temptation that comes to these young Christians is, 'I must insist upon this and that; I am a Christian, I understand, and therefore it must be done as I say.' The spirit is already wrong. Your desire is to do what you regard as right: but what of these others? 'Conscience, I say, not thine own, but of the other also.' 'All things are lawful, but all things are not expedient.' What about the weaker brother? What about the one who is not Christian at all? Do you not give them any thought? Are you simply concerned that everything should be done in such a way that you emerge absolutely right, and have kept the letter of the law in every detail? That is the essence of Pharisaism! That is the spirit that 'tithes mint and rue and all manner of herbs, and forgets the weightier matters of the law, such as love and mercy'. May God grant us wisdom in these matters! I have seen so much harm done to the cause of Christ by failure at this point that I am giving it special emphasis. We must never act in a selfish, self-righteous spirit.

But let me add something further. The Christian is in an exceptionally advantageous position in these matters because as a Christian he should have an understanding of the difficulties of his parents. Take the case of non-Christian children coming into conflict with the opinion and the will of non-Christian parents. What happens? Immediately, it is a clash of personalities, a clash of the wills, and neither side has any understanding of the other. The child says, 'The parents have no right to say this'; and the parents look at their children and say, 'These children are impossible and altogether wrong.' Both sides are standing rigidly without any attempt to understand the opposing viewpoint. But that should never be true of the Christian. He has this great advantage over the non-Christian; as a Christian he should know why his parents cannot understand him and why they are behaving as they do. He does not merely regard them as difficult parents, he is not merely interested in their personalities. Instead, as a Christian he says, 'Of course they cannot help it, in a sense; it is very sad, it is very tragic, but I must not be annoyed with them, because they cannot possibly see it from the Christian position. They are not Christians, and for me to expect them to take the Christian view when they are not Christians is to ask them to do the impossible. I myself was once in that position, I was just as blind. Thank God, my eyes have been opened and I now see the right way; but they do not, therefore I must be sympathetic towards them, I must be patient, I must be understanding. I must make every concession I can, I must go as far as I can to meet them and to help them and to placate them.'

Such is the advantage enjoyed by the Christian. 'Children, obey your parents, in the Lord'; you have this understanding. Do not merely stand as one personality against another personality; see that it is the blindness of sin that is causing the trouble. Do not look at them simply as parents who are against you; see, rather, the sin that is coming in and causing the division. That is what our Lord meant in his teaching about 'bringing a sword' and causing this kind of division. We must not be surprised at it, but we must not react violently to it. We must approach it all in a spirit of understanding and of sympathy.

That leads to my last reason. Whatever you and I may do as Christians, whatever we may do as Christian children, whenever we may come up against this clash, this division, and feel that we are compelled even to say 'No' to our parents, we must be always sure that what is uppermost in our minds at that point is a concern for the souls of our parents. 'Honour thy father and mother.' The fact that you have now become Christians, and that they are not Christians, does not mean that you look down on them and treat them with contempt and disdain, and dismiss them. You are to honour them, and you can honour them most of all by being concerned about their souls. If as Christian people we do not have a concern in our spirits and in our hearts about the souls of those who are related to us in this most intimate relationship, then we are not obeying our parents, we are not 'honouring our father and mother' in the way the Scriptures indicate.

Let us therefore safeguard ourselves by these considerations from the glib, superficial, mechanical kind of behaviour that is so often recommended to us, if not actually imposed upon us, by well-meaning but ignorant Christian people. There are many such. They say, 'Now you are converted, this is what you do now', and they almost encourage you to run against your own parents. Never allow them to do so. These fundamental rules and laws abide and remain. The only division that is legitimate is the one that is caused by Christ himself. We must never create divisions; we must do our utmost to avoid them, and must go to the uttermost limit to avoid them. The only lawful division is that inevitable, tremendous division that is made by the sword of the Spirit wielded by the Son of God himself, our Lord and Saviour Jesus Christ. We must never be difficult, we must never stand on irrelevant details; we must never do anything that causes division. The only division that is inevitable and allowable is that which is produced by the sword which our Lord said he had come to bring (*Matt.* 10:34–38).

We now turn our attention to the parents. 'Fathers', says the Apostle, 'Ye fathers, provoke not your children to wrath.' Notice that he mentions the fathers only. He has just quoted the words of the law, 'Honour thy father and mother', but now he singles out the fathers because the whole of his teaching has been, as we have seen, that the father is the one who is in the position of authority. That is what we always find in the Old Testament; that is how God has always taught people to behave; so he naturally addresses this particular injunction to the fathers. But the injunction is not to be confined to the fathers; it includes the mothers also; and at a time like the present we have reached a position in which the order almost has to be reversed! We are living in a kind of matriarchal society where fathers, alas, and husbands, have so abdicated their position in the home that almost everything is being left to the mothers. We have to realize therefore that what is said here to the fathers applies equally to the mothers. It applies to the one who is in the position of having to exercise discipline. In other words, what we are introduced to here in this fourth verse, and it is involved in the previous verse, is the whole problem of discipline.

We must examine this subject carefully, and it is of course a very extensive one. There is no subject, I would say once more, that is of such urgent importance in this country, and in every other country, as this whole problem of discipline. We are witnessing a breakdown in society, and it is mainly in connection with this matter of discipline. We have it in the home, we have it in the schools, we have it in industry; it is everywhere. The problem confronting society today in every walk of life is ultimately the problem of discipline. Responsibility, relationships, how life is to be conducted, how life is to proceed! The whole future of civilization, it seems to me, rests upon this. It is not the primary business of preaching to deal with political and social questions, though we can throw a most important light upon them.

We are told that the most important division in the world today is that brought about by the 'Iron Curtain'. In view of that, I venture on this assertion, this prophecy: If the West goes down and is defeated, it will be for one reason only, internal rot. There is no problem of discipline on the other side because there is a dictatorship there, and therefore they will have efficiency. We do not believe in dictatorship; therefore there is nothing more important for us than the problem of discipline. If we continue to spend our lives in jollification, doing less and less work, demanding more and more money, more and more pleasure and so-called happiness, more and more indulgence of the lusts of the flesh, with a refusal to accept our responsibilities, there is but one inevitable result: complete and abject failure.

Why did the Goths and the Vandals and other barbarians conquer the ancient Roman Empire? Was it by superior military power? Of course not! Historians know that there is only one answer; the fall of Rome came by reason of the spirit of indulgence that had invaded the Roman world – the games, the pleasures, the baths. The moral rot that had entered into the heart of the Roman Empire was the cause of Rome's 'decline and fall'. It was not superior power from the outside, but internal rot that was Rome's ruination. And the really alarming fact today is that we are witnessing a similar declension in this, and most other Western countries. This slackness, this indiscipline, the whole outlook and spirit is characteristic of a period of decadence. The pleasure mania, the sports mania, the drink and drug mania have gripped the masses. This is the essential problem, this sheer absence of discipline and of order and of true notions of government!

These matters, it seems to me, are raised very clearly by what the Apostle tells us here. I shall proceed to present these further to view, and to show how the Scripture enlightens us in regard to them. But before doing so, let me mention something that will assist and stimulate your whole process of thinking. One of our problems today is that we no longer do our own thinking. Newspapers do it for us, the people interviewed on radio and television do it for us, and we sit back and listen. That is one of the manifestations of the breakdown of self-discipline.

We must learn to discipline our minds. So I will give two quotations of Scripture, one on the one side, and one on the other side of this whole position. The problem of discipline lies between the two. Here is the limit on one side: 'He that spareth his rod hateth his son' (*Prov.* 13:24). The other is, 'Fathers, provoke not your children to wrath.' The whole problem of discipline lies between those two limits, and they are both found in the Scriptures.

Work the problem out in the Scriptures, try to get at the great scriptural principles that govern this vital, this urgent matter, this greatest problem confronting all the Western nations, if not also others, at this hour. All our problems result from our going to one extreme or the other. That is never found in Scripture. What characterizes the teaching of the Scriptures always and everywhere is their perfect balance, a fairness that never fails, the extraordinary way in which grace and law are divinely blended. We shall consider these matters in detail.

3. Discipline and the Modern Mind

W E CONTINUE OUR STUDY of what is one of the basic and fundamental matters concerning the whole of life and of conduct. It is a problem not only for Christian people, but for the whole of society. What particularly affects us who are Christian is this, that we are set, as the Scriptures remind us, as 'lights in the world', as 'the salt' of society, and like 'a city set upon a hill'. There is no hope for the world apart from the light which comes to it from the Christian teaching. It is therefore doubly important that as Christian people we should be careful to observe and to understand the apostolic teaching. It is for us to give an example to the whole world as to how life is to be truly lived. And we have a unique opportunity, I feel, at such a time as this for showing the Christian, biblical, balanced view concerning this vexed problem of discipline.

This urgent problem is not confined, of course, to the problem of children. The same principle is involved in the modern attitude to crime and to war and to punishment in every shape and form; it is a part of that same larger and general problem. But here we are looking at it in particular as it affects the discipline of children and the discipline of the home. We have seen that there are two fundamental statements which seem to govern any true thinking about this question of discipline. On the one hand you have the familiar statement 'Spare the rod and spoil the child', or the other forms of that statement which are found at various points in the book of Proverbs and in the Old Testament 'Wisdom' literature. That is one side. The other side is, 'Fathers, provoke not your children to wrath.' There are the two fundamental positions. Within the ellipse between these two foci we shall find the biblical doctrine concerning this subject.

We shall look at it first of all in general. What strikes us at once is the great change that has taken place during the present century with regard to this whole problem of discipline, and especially during the last thirty years or so. But it has been going on during the whole of this century. There has been a complete revolution in the attitude of people towards this matter.

Formerly we had what people today like to call derisively the Victorian outlook with regard to this matter of discipline. Let us admit quite readily and frankly that there is no question at all but that that was excessive. It was repressive, it was often brutal, indeed it can be said that sometimes it was even inhuman. The Victorian father, the Victorian grandfather, is a well-known and a well-recognized type. There was an element, indeed a considerable element, of the tyrant in their conception of fatherhood and of family discipline. The children were ruled severely and sternly, and the saying was, 'Children are to be seen and not heard.' That idea was certainly put into operation. Children were not allowed to express their opinion, they were frequently not allowed to ask questions; they were told what to do, and they had to do it; and if they refused they were punished with very great severity. We need not spend our time with this; it has been attacked and ridiculed and caricatured so much that everybody, surely, is familiar with that picture. Most of us probably are not old enough to remember it in actual practice, except those who are beyond, say, the age of sixty; but we are all familiar with the general picture and idea. That was the position about a hundred years ago and it continued more or less until the First World War.

But since then there has been an entire change; and today we are confronted by a position which is almost its exact opposite, for now we are tending to do away with discipline altogether. It is, as I have said, a part of a general attitude towards war, towards crime, towards punishment as a whole, and especially corporal and capital punishment.

A new climate of opinion has come in, which *in toto* rejects the ideas that constituted the Victorian outlook. Indeed we can describe it as a general opposition to the whole idea of justice, and of righteousness, of wrath and of punishment. These terms are all abominated and are hated. In general, the modern man dislikes them radically. We find this exemplified in our newspapers, in observable tendencies in Acts of Parliament, and in the changes that have been introduced increasingly. These great terms: right, truth, justice, righteousness, are rarely heard. The much-used words of today are peace, happiness, enjoyment, ease, tolerance. The modern man has revolted against the great terms that have always characterized the heroic ages in man's history, but that is very largely a reaction against the severities of the Victorian age.

What makes the position so serious is that this attitude is generally presented in terms of Christianity, and especially in terms of the New Testament teaching, and this, in particular, as contrasted with the Old Testament teaching. The case is often put thus, 'Of course the trouble with those Victorians was, as it was with the Puritans, that they lived in the Old Testament, they worshipped the God of the Old Testament. But', they add, 'of course we no longer believe that; theirs was only a tribal God; that is not the God of the Christian, that is not the "Father" of Jesus.' They claim that these modern ideas concerning discipline are based upon the New Testament, and that they have the true New Testament conception of God. They are therefore not interested, they say, in justice and righteousness, wrath and punishment. Nothing matters but love and understanding.

This is the point at which it all becomes so serious. And it is interesting to notice that men who do not even claim to be Christians are saying this kind of thing. You can even read statements in books and articles and journals which do not hesitate to assert that the Christian position is generally being put today, not by the church, but by some of the popular infidel writers, who are openly and frankly not Christian at all. We are told that the Christian case is going by default, that the church is not putting it forward, and that Christianity is really being presented today by men who are outside the church. It is said that they are giving the true exposition of the New Testament teaching as over against the Old Testament teaching. There exists this curious alliance of some people who call themselves Christians, and others who openly assert that they are not Christians; but together they agree that Christianity and the New Testament teach this modern view with regard to discipline, and that they therefore have departed from the former Victorian view, and particularly the Old Testament view.

Summing it up, we can say that the basic idea underlying this view is that human nature is essentially good. That is the fundamental philosophy. What is needed therefore is to draw out, to encourage, and to develop the child's personality. So there must be no repelling, no control; there must be no punishing, and no administering of correction because that tends to be repressive. That being the controlling principle, it naturally works out all along the line in every department of life.

Take, for instance, teaching methods. This is surely one of the most urgent matters confronting this country today. Teaching methods during the last twenty years or so have been determined almost entirely by this new outlook, by this new psychology which regards human nature as essentially good. The idea is that you must not compel or coerce the child. One of the first to describe this teaching was a Dr Maria Montessori whose method of teaching roughly came to this, that you should allow children to decide for themselves, and choose for themselves, what they want to learn. Before her days, of course, there had been a compulsory method of teaching the three Rs and you had to use it whether you wanted to or not. Children had to learn multiplication tables, and much else, by heart. It was done mechanically, there was no attempt to make it interesting to the children. They were simply told that they had to learn their Alphabet, their Tables, and their Grammar. All was drummed into them, and they had to repeat it mechanically until they knew it by memory and could repeat it by rote.

Now all that, we are told, is quite wrong because it did not develop the child's personality. Teaching must be made interesting, and everything must be explained to him. He must not learn in a mechanical manner, but must understand what he is learning; so the explanations are given. The old method has been discarded in terms of this new view of human nature, this whole attitude towards life which claims to be Christian. Thus in the matter of educational theory and method there has been this profound revolution. By now we are beginning to discover some of its results. You find industrialists and others complaining that many who apply for posts as clerks and typists can no longer spell or do simple arithmetic. But my concern is not with the practical and economic results but with the underlying principles.

Again, with respect to the question of punishment, this too has very largely become a thing of the past. We are told that you must not punish; you must appeal to children, show them the wrong, set them a good example, and then reward them positively. We must grant, of course, that there is a measure of truth in all this, but the danger is that men usually go from one extreme to the other, and by today the whole notion of punishment has largely vanished. Indeed there are some who would press this notion so far as to say that you should never punish a child. Some even say that the thing to do if a child does anything wrong is take the punishment upon yourself, and thereby you will shame the child, and lead him to give up his wrong and evil practice. I remember very well some thirty years ago a man who literally put this into practice in his own family. He had a child, who, like every other child, was given occasionally to disobedience and to doing wrong things; but this man having got hold of this new theory, decided that he would no longer punish the child in any shape or form, but take the punishment on himself. For instance, instead of punishing the child, he, the father, would not eat his supper on the night of the offence. The experiment, I must add, did not last long. In the interests of his own health he soon had to return to the old method!

That is a typical illustration of the modern attitude. Human nature, it is claimed, is essentially good, and you have but to appeal to that which is best and highest in it. You need never punish, you need never restrain, you need never exercise discipline. You have but to state the ideal, and suffer in yourself the punishment of wrong-doing in others, and the offenders will respond. People of this type believed that if you acted in that way with Hitler there would be no war; you could change Hitler if you just went and spoke nicely and kindly to him, and showed him how you were ready to suffer. There was a very popular preacher in London before the Second World War who actually proposed that he and a few others should go and stand between the armies of Japan and China that were fighting at that time. They did not actually do it, but they were quite convinced that if they but went and stood there between the rival armies, and sacrificed themselves, the war would end at once.

All this, I repeat, is based upon the notion that human

nature is essentially good; so you have only to appeal to it. You will never need to resort to punishment. And if you do punish at all, it must never be corporal, and it must never be punitive; if there is any sort of punishment, we are told, it must be reformatory. This is an interesting point. The new notion is that the business of punishment, if as much as this can be said in its favour, is to reform, not to exercise retribution. We are told that we must always be positive, that we must always be aiming at building up a new type of personality and of character.

How does it work out? Take the question of prisons. The modern notion is that the business of prisons is not to punish offenders but to reform them. So we are being told increasingly that what is needed in prisons is the abolition of restrictions and punishments. We must abolish the 'cat' and every form of corporal punishment, and the prisons must be manned by psychiatrists. A prison is a place in which a man should receive psychological and psychiatric treatment. You must not punish the prisoner for what he has done because essentially he is a good man. What you must do is to build up the goodness that is in him, and to draw it out. Show him the evil and wrong of certain of his own ideas, and of what he has been doing against society, and he will soon come to acknowledge his errors and to forsake them. The great need is to build up 'the other side'. And so by means of psychiatric treatment you will be reforming the man and building up his character and personality.

Such is the controlling idea today with regard to the treatment of crime and its punishment. Capital punishment has been abolished, all forms of corporal punishment must be abolished, indeed any kind of severity must be abolished; the whole emphasis is on this treatment by psychiatry: the psychological approach, the building up, the working on this positive something that is there in human nature!

And, of course, the same idea comes into the handling of children. The whole tendency today, if a child does not behave himself in school as he should, is to send him to a child psychiatrist; everybody must be treated psychologically. Essentially they are all good; therefore you must never punish. The rod, the cane, must be scrapped. What is needed is to draw out this inherent hidden good. So when the teacher fails to maintain discipline the child is sent off to the psychiatrist, the child psychologist, for investigation, and the prescribing of the appropriate treatment.

The point I am making is that all this is being done in the name of Christianity, and with the plea that it is New Testament as against Old Testament. This, we are told, is the approach of Christ towards these matters. In many senses, therefore, the whole Christian position is involved at this point, and the whole future of the church. Here is a view that infidels are advocating and supporting, as well they might, but it is being done in the name of Christianity and of the New Testament.

Let us examine this question further. What is the biblical, the Christian teaching with regard to this matter? I do not hesitate to assert that the biblical and Christian attitude towards these two extremes is that they are both wrong; that the Victorian position was wrong, and that the modern position is wrong, even more so. But we are concerned especially with the present and the prevailing argument. I shall return later to the Victorian notion, which can be dealt with in terms of this exhortation, 'Ye fathers, provoke not your children to wrath'; for that is exactly what they did; and this modern attitude is so much reaction to that. But let us look at the modern position first.

My first reason for asserting that, from the biblical and Christian standpoint, this modern notion with regard to the problem of discipline is completely wrong is that the opposite of a wrong type of discipline is surely not to have no discipline at all. Yet that is what is happening today. The Victorians, we are told, were wrong; so let there be literally no discipline at all, no punishment; allow the child to do as he likes, and almost everyone else to do as he likes. There is a fundamental fallacy here. The opposite of wrong discipline is not the absence of discipline, but right discipline, true discipline. That is what we find here in Ephesians chapter 6. 'Children, obey your parents in the Lord', and 'Ye fathers, provoke not your children to wrath.' Discipline them, yes, but do not let it be a wrong discipline; let it be the right sort of discipline. 'Do not provoke them to wrath, but bring them up in the nurture and admonition of the Lord.' Now that is true discipline. But the tragedy of today, with its superficial thinking, is to assume that the opposite of wrong discipline is no discipline at all. That is a complete fallacy from the standpoint of mere thought and philosophy, if from no other standpoint.

Or let me put the matter in another way. Any position which says 'law only' or which says 'grace only' is of necessity wrong, because in the Bible you have 'law' and 'grace'. It is not 'law or grace', it is 'law and grace'. There was grace in the Old Testament law. All the burnt offerings and sacrifices are indicative of that. It was God who ordered them. Let no one ever say that there was no grace in the law of God as given to Moses and the children of Israel. It is ultimately based on grace, it is law with grace in it.

And on the other hand we must never say that grace means lawlessness; that is Antinomianism, which is everywhere condemned in the New Testament. There were some early Christians who said, 'Ah, we are no longer under law, we are under grace; that means that what we do does not matter. Because we are no longer under law but are under grace, let us sin that grace may abound! Let us do what we like, it does not matter. God is love, we are forgiven, we are in Christ, we are born again, so let us do anything we like.' These false deductions are dealt with in the Epistles to the Romans and to the Corinthians and to the Thessalonians, and also in the first three chapters of the book of Revelation. It is a tragic fallacy to think that when you have grace there is no element of law at all, but that it is a kind of licence. That is a contradiction of the biblical teaching concerning both law and grace. There is grace in law, there is law in grace. We are not 'without law' as Christians, says Paul, but we are 'under law to Christ' (*1 Cor.* 9:21).

Of course there is discipline! In fact the Christian ought to be much more disciplined than the man who is under the law, because he sees its meaning more clearly, and he has greater power. He has a truer understanding, and should therefore live a better and a more disciplined life. There is not less discipline in the New Testament than in the Old; there is more, and at a deeper level. And in any case, as the Apostle Paul teaches in writing to the Galatians, you must not dismiss the law, for the law was 'our schoolmaster to bring us to Christ' (3:24). Do not set up these things as opposites. The law was given by God in order that men might be shut up and shut in, as it were, to Christ, who was to come, who was to give them this great salvation.

I assert, therefore, that this modern idea completely misunderstands both law and grace. It is a complete muddle, it is utter confusion; indeed it is not biblical at all. It is nothing but human philosophy, human psychology. It uses Christian terms but it really evacuates such terms of their real meaning.

Thirdly, the modern teaching, and this is one of the serious things concerning it, displays a complete misunderstanding of the biblical doctrine of God. This is the desperately serious thing. Modern man does not take his picture of God from the Bible; he takes it from his own brain and heart. He does not believe in 'revelation'. That is why he began the so-called Higher-criticism of the Bible about one and a half centuries ago.

Man has been creating a god in his own image, a god who must be the exact antithesis of the Victorian father. I am quoting the description from an eminent writer of the present century. 'Do you not see', he writes, 'that the God of the Old Testament is your Victorian father; and that that is all wrong?' So the Old Testament is virtually shed. 'The God we believe in', men say, 'is the God and Father of our Lord Jesus Christ.' But the Lord Jesus Christ believed in the God of the Old Testament. He said, 'Think not that I am come to destroy the law, or the prophets: I am not come to destroy, but to fulfil.' He believed in the God who gave a revelation of himself to Moses on the mount, and in the Ten Commandments. Our Lord believed and accepted all the Old Testament teaching.

The moderns have no right to claim that the new line is Christ's. It is not his teaching; it is their own teaching. The God who has revealed himself to us through the Bible is a God who is holy. It is the New Testament as well as the Old that tells us that we must approach God 'with reverence and godly fear, for our God is a consuming fire' (*Heb.* 12:29, quoting *Deut.* 4:24). Indeed the New Testament teaches that in the Old Testament we are given only a dim notion of the holiness, the majesty and the glory and the greatness of God. There, it was only an external representation. God is infinitely holy. 'God is light, and in him is no darkness at all.' God is righteous, God is always just. God is love, I know, but God is also all these other things; and there is no contradiction in them. They are all one, and they are all present at the same time, and in eternal power and fullness, in the Godhead.

That is the revelation of the Scripture. And the notion that God is One who can wink at sin and pretend that he has not seen it, and cover it over and forgive every offender, and never feel any wrath, and never punish is, I say, not only to deny the Old Testament, but to deny the New Testament also. It is the Lord Jesus Christ who spoke about the place 'where their worm dieth not, and the fire is not quenched'. It is he who tells us about the division of the sheep from the goats; it is he who says to certain men, 'Depart from me. I never knew you'; 'Depart unto the place prepared for the devil and his angels.'

Nothing could be more monstrous than that this modern teaching should masquerade under the name of the New Testament and of the Lord Jesus Christ. It is a denial of the biblical doctrine of God, as found in both Testaments. God is a holy God, a just God, a righteous God, who has made it plain that he will punish sin and transgression, and who has done so in history many times. He punished his own children of Israel for their transgressions; he sent them into captivity; he raised up the Assyrians and the Chaldeans as his instruments of chastisement of them. The Apostle Paul teaches explicitly in the Epistle to the Romans (1:18–32), that God punishes sin, and does so sometimes by abandoning the world to its own evil and iniquity. And it is becoming increasingly clear that he is doing so at this present hour, but that men blinded by modern psychology cannot see it, for they do not understand the biblical truth about God.

Why is the world in such trouble? Why are we all, as it were, trembling as to what is going to happen next? Why are we all alarmed about these terrible new armaments and the possibility of an atomic war? The explanation, I suggest, is that God is punishing us by abandoning us to ourselves, because we have refused to submit to him and to his holy and righteous laws. Our departure from the biblical teaching concerning God, and, as a consequence of that, from the whole revealed truth concerning discipline and government and order, has resulted in the very punishment to which men are so blind.

In the fourth place there is a complete failure to realize what sin has done to man. The modern notions that man is fundamentally and essentially good, and that, if only the good is drawn out, everything will be right; that you have only to make an appeal, and never punish, but simply take the suffering upon yourself, that offenders will be so moved by it, and so broken down by the moral appeal that you are putting to them, that they will stop doing wrong and begin to behave well; all these notions, I say, are the consequence of the rejection of the biblical doctrine of sin. The simple answer to them is that man's nature is evil, that, as the result of the Fall, he is altogether evil. He is a rebel, he is lawless, he is governed by wrong forces, and therefore he is impervious to all appeals that may come to him.

The modern world is proving it by bitter experience. The modern method has been tried now for a number of years. But what of the results? Mounting problems: juvenile delinquency, disorder in the home, theft, violence, murders, robbery, and the whole of modern society in confusion! The new theory has been given a good trial for thirty years and more, and the resulting problems are mounting up from week to week and almost from day to day. But nothing else is to be expected! Man is not fundamentally good. 'All the imaginations of the thoughts of his heart are only evil continually', as we are told they were in the days before the Flood (*Gen.* 6:5). Man is not a good creature who only needs a little encouragement; his nature is twisted and perverted and vile. He is a rebel, he hates the light, he loves the darkness, he is a creature of lust and passion. And it is the failure to recognize this that is responsible for this modern disastrous notion.

But in the fifth place, there is also a complete misunderstanding of the doctrine of the atonement and of redemption, and of the cardinal doctrine of regeneration. I still have to meet a pacifist who understands the doctrine of the atonement! I still have to meet the man who holds the modern view about discipline and punishment who understands the doctrine of the atonement. The biblical doctrine of the atonement tells us that, on the cross of Calvary, the just and holy and righteous God was punishing sin in the person of his own Son, that he might 'be just, and the justifier of him that believeth in Jesus' (*Rom.* 3:25–26). 'God hath laid on him the iniquity of us all' (*Isa.* 53:6). 'God hath made him to be sin for us who knew no sin, that we might be made the righteousness of God in him' (2 *Cor.* 5:21). 'By his stripes we are healed' (*1 Pet.* 2:24). 'It

hath pleased the Lord to bruise him' (*Isa.* 53:10). The justice
and the righteousness of God demanded this, the wrath of God
upon sin insisted upon this. But this is where we see truly the
love of God, that it is so great that the wrath is poured out even
on his own Son in all his innocence, in order that you and I
might be rescued and delivered. But the moderns do not
understand or believe in atonement. They see nothing but
sentimentality in the cross; they see cruel soldiers putting to
death the Son of God who nevertheless smiles upon them and
says, 'I still forgive you though you have done this to me.'

That is what they say; but the Bible does not teach that. It is
full of teaching concerning burnt offerings and sacrifices, of the
necessity for the shedding of sacrificial blood, and that
'without shedding of blood there is no remission (of sins)'
(*Heb.* 9:22). That is the teaching of the Old Testament and the
New, and this modern idea is a complete denial of it. Punishment is taught everywhere; and you see it supremely on the
cross on Calvary's hill.

Or take the doctrine of regeneration. If man is essentially
good he does not need to be 'born again', he does not need
regeneration. But regeneration is a central doctrine in the Bible;
our only hope is that we be made 'partakers of the divine
nature'. Thus this new teaching is a denial of the fundamental
biblical doctrines, and yet it comes and masquerades in the
name of Christianity. The biblical teaching is that until a man
comes 'under grace' he has to be kept 'under law', that sin and
evil must be kept within bounds. And God has done that! Who
has appointed magistrates? God! Read Romans 13. 'The
magistrate', we are told there, 'beareth not the sword in vain.'
Who has appointed kings and governors? God! Who has
appointed states? God! To keep sin and evil within bounds. If
he had not done so the world would have putrefied to nothing
centuries ago. God has instituted law because of man's sinful
nature, and in order that man may be restrained and kept from
evil until he comes 'under grace'. It is God who, in the days of

Moses, gave the law, and he gave it for that reason. And obviously if a law is to be effective it must have sanctions. There is no value in having a law if, when a man is arrested in enforcement of the law, you immediately tell him, 'Well, do not feel troubled, we have arrested you, but there is no punishment.' Would that be effective?

There is surely a contemporary illustration that ought to satisfy our minds with regard to this matter. Consider the slaughter that is taking place on the roads. What is being done about it? The authorities are making appeals, issuing statements, bringing in new regulations, getting the radio and the television to keep on repeating warnings, especially before Easter and Christmas. But do they have any effect? Very little! Why? Because man is a rebel, because he is naturally lawless. There is only one way in which the State can deal with this problem, and that is, by the punishment of offenders. That is the only language they can understand. Man in sin never has understood any other language. Go to him in a spirit of sweet reasonableness and he will take advantage of you.

The British government tried that method with Hitler; we called it appeasement. If we can see that it was wrong there, why cannot we see that it is wrong with all other individuals? There is no purpose in making appeals in terms of sweet reasonableness to men who are evil and governed by lust and passion.

The biblical teaching is that such people are to be punished, and are to feel their punishment. If they will not listen to the law, then the sanctions of the law are to be applied. God, when he gave his law, accompanied it by the sanctions which were to be applied following transgression. When the law was broken the sanctions were carried out. God does not give a law and say that disobedience to its requirements does not matter. God carries out his law. And as you look at the history of this country, not to look further afield, you will always find that the most disciplined and the most glorious periods in that history have been the periods that have followed a religious reformation. Look at the Elizabethan period following the Protestant Reformation, when men brought the Bible back, Old Testament and New Testament, and put it into practice, and enforced their laws.

The Elizabethan period, the Cromwellian period, and the period following the Evangelical Awakening of the eighteenth century all illustrate the biblical principle. The biblical teaching is that because man is a fallen creature, because he is a sinner and a rebel, because he is a creature of lust and passion, and governed by them, he must be forcibly restrained, he must be kept in order. The principle applies alike to children and to adults who are guilty of misdemeanour and crime and a departure from the law of the land and from the law of God. Try any other method and you will have a return to chaos, as we are already beginning to experience. The biblical teaching, founded upon the character and being of God, and recognizing that man is in a state of sin, requires that law must be enforced, in order that men may be brought to see and to know God; next that they may be brought into grace; so that finally they may be brought to own and obey the higher law under which they delight in pleasing God and honouring and keeping his holy commandments.

We must start therefore with this principle that the biblical teaching everywhere is that there must be discipline, there must be punishment. But then that leaves us with this question: How, exactly, is that punishment to be meted out, and particularly in the Christian home? And it is there that our text is so important. You must exercise discipline, but you must not 'provoke your children to wrath'. There is a wrong way of exercising discipline as well as a right way, and what we shall be concerned about further is to discover the right, the true, the biblical method of exercising the discipline which is commanded us by the holy law of God. The modern notion, although it often claims the name of Christ, is a denial of all the basic and fundamental doctrines of the Christian faith. It is not surprising that infidels are advocating it very loudly with respect to capital punishment, to war, to education, to prison reform, and much else. It is not surprising, I say, that they are advocating it, because we do not expect Christian and biblical understanding of them. But a Christian should and must understand.

4. Balanced Discipline

WE COME NOW TO THE QUESTION of the administration of discipline. The Apostle deals with that, in particular, in Ephesians 6:4. There is no question about the need of discipline, and that it must be enforced. But how is that to be done? It is here that a great deal of confusion has often arisen. We have agreed already that, beyond question, our Victorian grandfathers were guilty of error at this point, and that they frequently did not exercise discipline in the right and the biblical way and manner. We see also that what we have today is largely a violent reaction against that. That does not justify the present position, but it does help us to understand it. What is important is that we must not fall into the error of reverting again from the present position to that other extreme which was equally wrong. And here, if we but follow the Scripture we shall have a balanced view. Discipline is essential and must be enforced; but the Apostle exhorts us to be very careful as to how we exercise it, because we can do more harm than good if we do not do it in the right way.

In general, of course, there is very little need of this teaching at the present time, because, as I have been indicating, the trouble today is that people do not believe in discipline at all. There is little need, therefore, to tell them not to exercise discipline in the wrong way. We have to urge the modern man to recognize the need of discipline and to put it into practice.

But in the realm of the church, and perhaps in the realm of evangelical Christians in particular, and especially in the U. S.A., what the Apostle says in this fourth verse will be needed more and more. That need arises in this way. The ever-present danger is to react too violently. It is always wrong when our attitude is determined by another attitude which we regard as wrong.

Our view should never result from a merely negative reaction. This principle is true not only with respect to this particular subject, but in many realms and departments of life. Far too often we allow our attitude to be governed and determined by something that is wrong. Let me give one present-day illustration of this tendency. There are Christians in certain parts of the world who are reacting so violently to a wrong kind of fundamentalism at the present time that they are almost losing their hold of essential Christian doctrine. It is their annoyance with something that is wrong that determines their position. That is always wrong. Our position must always be determined positively by the Scriptures. We must not merely be reactionaries. And in this particular matter of discipline in the home, and of children, there is a very real danger that good evangelical Christians, having seen clearly that the modern attitude is entirely and utterly wrong, and being determined not to accept it, may go to the other extreme and revert to the old Victorian idea. They therefore need the exhortation which we find in these verses of our Epistle.

The Apostle divides his teaching into two sections, the negative and the positive. This problem he says is not confined to the children; the fathers, the parents, have also to be careful. Negatively, he tells them, 'Provoke not your children to wrath.' Positively, he says, 'But bring them up in the nurture and the admonition of the Lord.' As long as we remember both aspects, all will be well.

We start with the negative, 'Provoke not your children to wrath.' These words can be translated, 'Do not exasperate your children, do not irritate your children, do not provoke your children to become resentful.' That is always a very real danger when we exercise discipline. And if we become guilty of it we shall do much more harm than good. We shall not have succeeded in disciplining our children, we shall simply have produced such a violent reaction in them, so much wrath and resentment, that the position will be worse, almost, than if we had not exercised any discipline at all. But as we have seen, both extremes are altogether wrong. In other words we must exercise this discipline in such a manner that we do not irritate our children or provoke them to a sinful resentment. We are required to keep the balance.

How is this to be done? How is such discipline to be exercised by parents? And not by parents only, but by school-teachers, or anyone who is in the position of having charge and control of those who are younger than themselves. Once more we must go back to chapter 5, verse 18. 'Be not drunk with wine wherein is excess, but be filled with the Spirit.' That is always the key. We saw when we were dealing with that verse that the life lived in the Spirit, the life of a man who is filled with the Spirit, is characterized always by two main things – power and control. It is a disciplined power. Remember how Paul puts it in writing to Timothy. 'God', he says, 'hath not given us the spirit of fear, but of power, and of love and of a sound mind (discipline)' (2 *Tim.* 1: 8). Not uncontrolled power, but power controlled by love and a sound mind, discipline! That is always the characteristic of the life of a man who is 'filled with the Spirit'.

In other words, the Christian is entirely unlike the man who is under the influence of wine, the man who is besotted with wine. There is always excess in that case and the man reacts violently. You can easily irritate a drunken man and provoke him to a violent reaction. He lacks balance, he has no judgment, he takes great offence at a triviality, and on the other hand is much too pleased about something which in itself is trivial. He is invariably guilty of excessive reaction. But the Christian, says the Apostle, is always to manifest the antithesis of that type of behaviour.

How, then, am I to exercise this discipline? 'Provoke not your children to wrath.' This is to be the first principle governing our action. We are incapable of exercising true discipline unless we are first able to exercise self-control, and discipline our own tempers. The trouble with a man who is 'drunk with wine' is that he cannot control himself; he is being controlled by his instincts and passions and lower nature. Alcohol puts out of action the higher centres of the brain, including the sense of control. It is one of those depressant drugs that knocks out the finer discriminating abilities of the brain, the highest centres of all, with the result that the instinctual, the elemental elements come out. That is what happens to the man who is drunk with wine, hence his excess and lack of control. But Christians are to be filled with the Spirit, and people who are filled with the Spirit are always characterized by control.

When you are disciplining a child, you should have first controlled yourself. If you try to discipline your child when you are in a temper, it is certain that you will do more harm than good. What right have you to say to your child that he needs discipline when you obviously need it yourself? Self-control, control of temper is an essential prerequisite in the control of others. But that is the trouble, is it not? We see it on the streets, everywhere. We see parents administering chastisement in a rage, often trembling in a temper. They have no self-control, and the result is that the child is exasperated.

So the very first principle is that we must start with ourselves. We must be certain that we are in control of ourselves, that we are cool. Whatever may have happened, whatever the provocation, we must not react with the violence similar to that of the man who is drunk; there must be this personal discipline, this self-control that enables a man to look at the situation objectively, and to deal with it in a balanced and controlled manner. How important this is! The nations need to learn this very lesson. Their conferences break down because men behave like children or worse; they cannot control themselves, they react violently. This 'drunken' condition, these violent reactions, are a cause of war. They are the chief causes of all the breakdowns in life, in marriage, in the home, and in every other sphere. But nowhere is this lesson more important than in the realm of disciplining our children.

The second principle arises, in a sense, out of the first. If a parent is to exercise this discipline in the right way he must never be capricious. There is nothing more irritating to the one who is undergoing discipline than a feeling that the person who is administering it is capricious and uncertain. There is nothing more annoying to a child than the kind of parent whose moods and actions you can never predict, who is changeable, whose condition is always uncertain.

There is no worse type of parent than he who one day, in a kindly mood, is indulgent and allows the child to do almost anything it likes, but who the next day flares up in a rage if the child does scarcely anything at all. That makes life impossible for the child. Capriciousness in the parent is again indicative of this 'drunk with wine' condition. The reactions of a drunken man are unpredictable; you cannot tell whether he is going to be in a genial mood or in a bad temper, he is not governed by reason, there is no control, there is no balance. Such a parent, I say again, fails to exercise a true and helpful discipline, and the position of the child becomes impossible. He is provoked and irritated to wrath, and has no respect for such a parent.

I am referring not only to temperamental reactions, but to conduct also. The parent who is not consistent in his conduct cannot truly exercise discipline in the case of the child. A parent who does one thing today, and the contrary thing tomorrow, is not capable of sound discipline. There must be consistency, not only in the reaction but also in the conduct and the behaviour of the parent; there must be a pattern about the life of the parent, for the child is always observing and watching. But if he observes that the parent is erratic and himself does the very thing that he forbids the child to do, again you cannot expect the child to benefit from any discipline administered by such a parent. There must be nothing erratic, capricious, uncertain or changeable in the parents if they are to exercise discipline.

Another most important principle is that the parents must never be unreasonable or unwilling to hear the child's case. There is nothing that so annoys the one who is being disciplined as the feeling that the whole procedure is utterly unreasonable. In other words, it is a thoroughly bad parent who will not take any circumstances into consideration at all, or who will not listen to any conceivable explanation. Some fathers and mothers, in the desire to exercise discipline, are liable to become utterly unreasonable, and they themselves may be very much at fault. The report they have received concerning the child may be wrong, or there may have been peculiar circumstances of which they are ignorant; but the child is not even allowed to state the position, or to give any kind of explanation. Of course one realizes that advantage can be taken of this by the child. All I am saying is that we must never be unreasonable. Let the explanation be given by the child, and if it is not a true reason, then you can chastise for that also, as well as for the particular act which constitutes the offence. But to refuse to listen, to prohibit any kind of reply, is inexcusable.

We are all clear about this principle when we see a state behaving in a wrong way. We do not like a police state, we are proud of the Habeas Corpus Act in this country, which says that it is a grievous wrong to keep a man in prison without giving him a trial. We wax eloquent about this, but very often in our homes we do exactly the same thing. The child is not given any opportunity at all to state his case, reason does not come into the situation for a moment, we refuse to grant even the possibility that there might be some explanation that we have not heard of hitherto. Such conduct is always wrong; that is to provoke our children to wrath. It is certain to exasperate and irritate them into a condition of rebellion and of antagonism.

But there is another principle to be considered: the parent must never be selfish. 'Parents, provoke not your children to wrath.' This happens sometimes because parents are guilty of just plain selfishness. My charge applies to persons who do not recognize that the child has his own life and personality, and who seem to think that children are entirely for their pleasure, or for their use.

They have an essentially wrong notion of parenthood and what it means. They do not realize that we are but guardians and custodians of these lives that are given to us, that we do not possess them, that they do not 'belong' to us, that they are not 'goods' or chattels, that we have no absolute right over them. But there are many parents who behave as if they had such a right of ownership; and the personality of the child receives no recognition. There is nothing more deplorable or reprehensible than a domineering parent. I am referring to the kind of parent who imposes his or her personality upon the child, and who is always crushing the child's personality; the type of parent who demands everything and who expects everything from the child. It is generally referred to as possessiveness. This is a most cruel attitude, and alas, it can persist into adult life.

Some of the greatest tragedies I have encountered in my pastoral experience have been due to this very thing. I know many people whose lives have been entirely ruined by selfish, possessive, domineering parents. I know many men and women who have never married for this reason. They were made to feel that they were well-nigh criminals because they even thought of leaving father or mother; their whole life was to be lived for the parents. For what had they come into the world if not for this? They were not allowed to have an independent life of their own, or to develop their own personality; a domineering father or mother had crushed out the life and the individuality and the personality of the son or daughter. That is not discipline; it is tyranny of the foulest type, and a contradiction of the plain teaching of Scripture. It is utterly inexcusable; and while it crushes the personality of the child, it breeds resentment. How can it fail to do so? Let us make sure that we are entirely free from that. 'Be not drunk with wine, wherein is excess.' The drunkard thinks of no one but himself, his one concern is his own satisfaction. If he thought of others he would never be drunk, because he knows that he brings suffering upon them. Drunkenness is a manifestation of selfishness, it is sheer selfish indulgence. We must not be guilty of that spirit in any respect, and particularly in this most delicate relationship of parents and children.

Yet again: Punishment, discipline, must never be administered in a mechanical manner. There are people who believe in discipline for its own sake. That is not the biblical teaching, but the philosophy of the Sergeant-Major. There is nothing to be said for it, it is unintelligent! That is the horrible thing about such discipline. In the Army and other armed Services it is unintelligent; it is done by numbers, personality is not considered at all. It may be necessary there, but when it comes into the realm of the home it, too, is something which is quite inexcusable. In other words, in order to administer discipline in the right and true way there must always be a reason for it; it is not to be applied in a mechanical manner. It must always be intelligent; there must always be a reason for it, and that reason should always be made plain and clear. It must never be thought of in terms of pressing a button and expecting an inevitable result to follow. That is not true discipline; it is not even human. That belongs to the realm of mechanics. But true discipline is always based on understanding; it has something to say for itself; it has an explanation to give.

Notice that all along we are finding it necessary to strike a balance. In criticizing the modern view which does not recognize discipline at all, we noted that it starts on the assumption that all you have to do is to give explanations, and make appeals, and all will be well. We saw clearly that that is not true in either theory or practice; but it is equally wrong to swing over to the other extreme and say, 'This has to be done because I say so. There is to be no questioning and there will be no explanation.' A Christian, balanced discipline is never mechanical; it is always living, it is always personal, it is always understanding, and above all it is always highly intelligent. It knows what it is doing, and it is never guilty of excess. It has not lost control of itself, it is not a kind of cataract pouring forth in an uncontrolled and violent manner. There is always this intelligent and understanding element at the very heart and centre of true discipline.

That leads inevitably to the sixth principle. Discipline must never be too severe. Here is perhaps the danger that confronts many good parents at the present time as they see the utter lawlessness about them, and as they rightly bemoan it and condemn it. Their danger is to be so deeply influenced by their revulsions as to go right over to this other extreme and to become much too severe. The opposite of no discipline at all is not cruelty, it is balanced discipline, it is controlled discipline. An ancient adage supplies a fundamental rule and law about this whole matter. It is that 'the punishment should fit the crime'. In other words, we must be careful that we do not administer the maximum punishment for all offences, great or small.

This is simply to say again that it must not be mechanical; for if the punishment meted out is disproportionate to the misdemeanour, the crime, or whatever it is, it cannot possibly do good. It will inevitably give the one who is punished a sense of injustice, a feeling that the punishment is so severe, so out of proportion to what was done that it constitutes an act of violence, not one of sane chastisement. That inevitably produces this 'wrath' of which the Apostle speaks. The child is irritated, he feels it is unreasonable. Though perhaps he is prepared to admit a measure of guilt he is quite sure that it was not as bad as all that. To put it in another way, we must never humiliate another person. If in punishing or administering discipline or correction, we are ever guilty of humiliating the child, it is clear that we ourselves need to be disciplined. Never humiliate! Certainly punish, if punishment is called for, but let it be a reasonable punishment based upon understanding. And never do it in such a way that the child feels that he is being trampled upon and being utterly humiliated in your presence, and still more, in the presence of others.

All this, I well know, can prove very difficult; but if we are 'filled with the Spirit' we shall have sound judgment in these matters. We shall learn that our administering of discipline must never be merely a means of giving relief to our own feelings. That is always wrong; and we must never allow ourselves to be governed by a delight in punishing; nor, as I have stressed, must we trample upon the personality and the life of the individual with whom we are dealing. The Spirit warns us to be extremely careful at this point. The moment personalities are left out, and this rigid, hard and harsh idea of punishment comes in, we are guilty of the very things against which Paul warns us. We are indeed provoking and irritating our children to wrath and we are making rebels of them. We are losing their respect, we make them feel they are hardly done by; a sense of injustice rankles within them, and they feel that we are being cruel. That benefits neither one party nor the other, and so we must never attempt discipline in that way.

So we come to what is, in many ways, the last of our negatives. We must never fail to recognize growth and development in the child. This is another alarming parental defect which, thank God, one does not see now so often as formerly. But there are still some parents who continue to regard their children all their lives as if they had never out-grown their childhood. The children may be twenty-five, but they still treat them as if they were five. They do not recognize that this person, this individual, this child whom God has given them in His grace, is one that is growing and developing and maturing. They do not recognize that the child's personality is blossoming forth, that knowledge is being gained, that experience is being widened, and that the child is developing even as they themselves have done. This is of particular importance at the stage of adolescence; hence one of the major social problems of today is the handling and the treatment of the adolescent. It is the problem of the Sunday schools as well as the day schools. Sunday school teachers testify that they have little difficulty until children come to adolescence, but that then they tend to lose them. Parents find the same thing. This period of adolescence is notoriously the most difficult age through which we all have to pass, and it therefore needs special grace and understanding, and the most careful handling.

As parents we must never be guilty of failing to recognize this factor, and we have to adjust ourselves to it. Because you are able to dominate your child, say up to the age of nine or ten years, you must not say, 'I am going to continue to do this, come what may. His will must be broken by mine. I care not what he may feel or what he understands, children know very little, so I shall continue to impose my will on him.' To think and to act in that way means you are certain to provoke your child to wrath, and thereby do him great harm. You will do the child psychological harm; you may even do him physical harm. You will create in him various types of psychosomatic illnesses which are so common at the present time. This kind of behaviour on the part of parents is prolific in the production of such effects and results. We must never be guilty of that.

'How do I avoid all these evils?', you ask. One good rule is
that we should never foist our views upon our children. Up to
a certain age it is right and good to teach them certain things
and insist upon them, and there will be no difficulty about that,
if done properly. They should even enjoy it. But shortly they
come to an age when they begin to hear other views and ideas
from their friends, probably in school or other associations.
Now a crisis begins to develop. The parents' whole instinct,
very rightly, is to protect the child, but it can be done in such a
way as, again, to do more harm than good. If you give the
impression to the child that he has to believe these things
simply because you believe them, and because your parents did
so, you will inevitably create a reaction. It is unscriptural to
do so. And not only is it unscriptural, but it betrays a dismal
lack of understanding of the New Testament doctrine of
regeneration.

An important principle arises at this point which applies not
only in this realm but in many other realms. I am constantly
having to tell people who have become Christian and whose
loved ones are not Christian, to be careful. They themselves
have come to see the Christian truth, and they cannot understand why this other member of the family, husband, wife,
father, mother, or child, fails to do so. Their whole tendency is
to be impatient with them and to dragoon them into the
Christian faith, to foist their belief upon them. This must on no
account be done. If the person in question is not regenerate he
or she cannot exercise faith. We need to be 'quickened' before
we can believe. When one is 'dead in trespasses and sins', one
cannot believe; so you cannot foist faith on others. They do not
see it, they do not understand it. 'The natural man receiveth
not the things of the Spirit of God, for they are foolishness unto
him; neither can he know them, for they are spiritually
discerned' (*1 Cor.* 2: 14).

Many parents have fallen into this error just at this point.
They have tried to dragoon their children in the adolescent

stage into the Christian faith; they have tried to foist their views on them, they have tried to compel them to say things that they do not really believe. This method is always wrong.

'Well, what can one do?', I shall be asked. Our business is to try to win them, to try to show them the excellence and the reasonableness of what we are and of what we believe. We must be very patient with them, and bear with their difficulties. They have their difficulties, though to you they are nothing. But to them they are very real. The whole art of exercising discipline is to recognize this other personality all the time. You must put yourself into his place, as it were, and with real sympathy and love and understanding try to help him. If the children refuse and reject your efforts, do not react violently, but give the impression that you are very sorry, that you are very grieved for their sakes, and that you feel they are missing something most precious. And at the same time you must make as many concessions as you can. You must not be hard and rigid, you must not refuse everything automatically without any reason, simply because you are the parent, and this is your method and manner.

On the contrary, you must be concerned to make every legitimate concession that you can, to go as far as you can in the matter of concession, thereby showing that you are paying respect to the personality and to the individuality of the child. That in and of itself is always good and right, and it will always result in good.

Let me summarize my argument. Discipline must always be exercised in love, and if you cannot exercise it in love do not attempt it at all. In that case you need to deal with yourself first. The Apostle has already told us to speak the truth in love in a more general sense; but exactly the same applies here. Speak the truth, but in love. It is precisely the same with discipline; it must be governed and controlled by love. 'Be not drunk with wine, wherein is excess, but be filled with the Spirit'. What is 'the fruit of the Spirit'? 'Love, joy, peace, longsuffering, gentleness, goodness, meekness, faith and temperance.' If, as parents, we are 'filled with the Spirit', and produce such fruit, discipline will be a very small problem as far as we are concerned. 'Love, joy, peace, longsuffering' – always in love, always for the child's good. The object of discipline is not to keep up your standard, or to say, 'I have decided that this is how it should be, and therefore it shall be so.' You must not think of yourself primarily, but of the child. The child's good is to be your controlling motive. You must have a right view of parenthood and regard the child as a life given to you by God. What for? To keep to yourself, and to mould to your pattern, to impose your personality upon it? Not at all! But put into your care and charge by God in order that his soul may ultimately come to know Him and to know the Lord Jesus Christ. The child is as much an entity as you are yourself, given, sent by God into this world even as you were. So you must look even at your own children primarily as souls, and not as you look at an animal that you happen to possess, or certain goods that you possess. This is a soul given to you by God, and you are to act as its guardian and custodian.

Finally, discipline must always be exercised in such a way as to lead children to respect their parents. They will not always understand, and they will probably feel at times that they do not deserve punishment. But if we are 'filled with the Spirit', the effect of our disciplining them will be that they will love us and respect us; and a day will come when they will thank us for having done it.

Even when they want to defend themselves there will be something within them that tells them that we are right. They will have a fundamental respect for our characters. They are watching our lives; they see the discipline and the control we exercise over ourselves, and they will see that what we do to them is not something capricious, that we are not merely giving vent to our own feelings and getting relief. They will always know that we love them, that we are concerned about their well-being and their benefit in this sinful, evil world; and so there will be this underlying respect and admiration and liking and love.

'And ye fathers, provoke not your children to wrath.' What a tremendous thing life is! How wonderful are all these relationships: husband, wife, parents, children! We see people in the world about us rushing into marriage and rushing out of marriage. As for the children, so many of them have no conception of what parenthood really means! Children to many are but a nuisance, over-fondled at one time, too severely punished at another; often left alone in their homes while the parents go out to 'enjoy' themselves; sent off to residential schools so that the parents may have their freedom! How little thought is given to the child, to his suffering, to the strain upon his sensitive nature! The tragedy of it all is that the lives of such people are not governed by the New Testament teaching; they are not 'filled with the Spirit'; they do not treat their children as God in His infinite love and kindness and compassion has treated us.

What if God dealt with us as we often deal with our children! Oh, the longsuffering of God! Oh, the patience of God! Oh, the amazing way in which He bears with our evil manners as He did with those of the children of Israel of old! There is nothing more amazing to me than the patience of God, and His longsuffering toward us. I say to Christian people, and all who are in any way responsible for the discipline of children and of young people, 'Let this mind be in you which was also in Christ Jesus.' And let the same love be in us also, lest we 'provoke our children to wrath' and thereby involve them and ourselves in all the evil consequences of our failure.

5. Godly Upbringing

WE HAVE SEEN that the Apostle's exhortation to the parents has two sides. There is the negative side which tells us that we must not do anything to exasperate our children, must not irritate them, must not provoke them; and then the positive side: 'Bring them up in the nurture and admonition of the Lord.' So we turn now to this positive side of the Apostle's injunction.

The very way in which Paul puts his exhortation is interesting: 'Bring them up', he says, and that is but another way of saying, 'Rear, nourish them to maturity.' In other words, the first thing that parents have to do is to realize their responsibility for the children. As we have emphasized, they are not our property, they do not ultimately belong to us, they are given to us by God for a while. For what purpose? Not that we may get what we want out of them, and use them simply to please ourselves, or to gratify our own desires. No, our business is to realize that they have to be 'reared', 'brought up', 'nurtured', 'prepared', not only for living their life in this world, but especially for the establishment of a right relationship of their souls to God.

These injunctions remind us of the greatness of life; and there is nothing more sad and tragic about the world today than the failure of the masses of the people to realize its greatness.

What a tremendous thing it is that we should exist and live as individuals! And when we consider the realm of the home and the family it becomes yet more wonderful. What a great conception the Apostle's teaching gives us of parenthood and its function! He tells us that we are given these children in order that we may bring them up and rear them and train them in the way they should go.

The newspapers are constantly reminding us of the care and the attention which people give to rearing various types of animals. It is not an easy thing to train an animal, whether it is a horse or a dog or any other. It demands much time and attention. The diet has to be considered, the exercises have to be planned, suitable bedding has to be provided; the animal has to be protected from various hazards; and so on. People pay large sums of money, spend a good deal of time, and give much thought to the bringing up and rearing of an animal that it may become a prize-winner in a show. But sometimes one is given the impression that very little time and care, attention and thought, are given to the rearing of children. That is one reason why the world is as it is today, and why we are confronted by acute social problems at this present time. If people but gave as much thought to the rearing of their children as they do to the rearing of animals and flowers, the situation would be very different. They read books and listen to talks about these other matters, and want to know exactly what they have to do. But how much time is given to the consideration of this great question of rearing children? It is taken for granted, done anyhow, and the consequences are painfully obvious.

If we are to carry out the Apostle's injunction, therefore, we must sit back for a moment, and consider what we have to do. When the child comes we must say to ourselves, we are the guardians and the custodians of this soul. What a dread responsibility! In business and in professions men are well aware of the great responsibility that rests upon them in the decisions they have to take. But are they aware of the infinitely greater responsibility they bear with respect to their own children? Do they give even the same amount of thought and attention and time to it, not to say more? Does it weigh as heavily upon them as the responsibility which they feel in these other realms? The Apostle urges us to regard this as the greatest business in life, the greatest matter which we ever have to handle and transact.

The Apostle does not stop at that: 'Bring them up', he says, 'in the nurture and admonition of the Lord.' The two words he uses are full of interest. The difference between them is, that the first, 'nurture', is more general than the second. It is the totality of nurturing, rearing, bringing up the child. It includes, therefore, general discipline. And, as all the authorities are agreed in pointing out, its emphasis is upon actions. The second word, 'admonition', has reference rather to words which are spoken.

'Nurture' is the more general term and includes everything that we do for the children. It includes the whole process in general of the cultivation of the mind and the spirit, the morals and the moral behaviour, the whole personality of the child. That is our task. It is to look upon the child and care for it, and guard it. We met this same term in Ephesians 5:29 when we were dealing with the relationship of husbands and wives, where we were told that the Lord himself 'nourisheth and cherisheth' the church. 'No man ever yet hated his own flesh, but nourisheth and cherisheth it, even as the Lord the church.' Here we are told to do the same with respect to our children.

The word 'admonition' carries much the same meaning, except that it puts greater emphasis upon speech. Thus there are two aspects of this matter. First we have to deal with general conduct and behaviour, the things we have to do by actions. Then, in addition, there are certain admonitions that should be addressed to the child, words of exhortation, words of encouragement, words of reproof, words of blame. Paul's term includes all these, indeed everything we say to the children in actual words when we are defining positions and indicating what is right or wrong, encouraging, exhorting, and so on. Such is the meaning of the word 'admonition'.

Children are to be reared in 'the nurture and the admonition' and then the most important addition of all, 'of the Lord'; 'the nurture and admonition of the Lord'. This is where Christian parents, engaged in their duty towards their children, are in an entirely different category from all other parents. In other words, this appeal to Christian parents is not simply to exhort them to bring up their children in terms of general morality or good manners or commendable behaviour in general. That, of course, is included; everyone should be doing it; non-Christian parents should be doing it. They should be concerned about good manners, good general behaviour, an avoidance of evil; they should teach their children to be honest, dutiful, respectful, and all these various things. That is but common morality, and Christianity has not started at that point. Even pagan writers interested in the good ordering of society have always exhorted their fellow men to teach such principles. Society cannot continue without a modicum of discipline and of law and order, at every level, and at every age. But the Apostle is not referring to that only; he says that the children of Christians are to be brought up 'in the nurture and admonition of the Lord'.

It is at this point that the peculiar and specific Christian thinking and teaching enter. In the forefront of the minds of Christian parents must ever be the thought that the children are to be brought up in the knowledge of the Lord Jesus Christ as Saviour and as Lord. That is the peculiar task to which Christian parents alone are called. This is not only their supreme task; their greatest desire and ambition for their children should be that they should come to know the Lord Jesus Christ as their Saviour and as their Lord. Is that our main ambition for our children? Does that come first? That they may come to know him, whom to know is life eternal (*John* 17:3), that they may know him as their Saviour and that they may follow him as their Lord? 'In the nurture and the admonition of the Lord'! These, then, are the terms the Apostle uses.

We now come to the practical question as to how this is to be done. Here, again, is a matter that needs our most urgent attention. In the Bible itself there is a great deal of emphasis laid upon child training. Take, for instance, words found in the sixth chapter of Deuteronomy. Moses has reached the end of his life, and the children of Israel are shortly to enter the promised land. He reminds them of the law of God and tells them how they are to live when they enter into the land of their inheritance. And among other things he is very careful to tell them that they have to teach their children the law. It is not enough that they know it and observe it themselves, they must pass on their knowledge. The children must be taught it, and must never forget it. So he repeats the injunction twice in that one chapter. It occurs again in chapter 11 of Deuteronomy, and frequently here and there throughout the Old Testament. It is found in the New Testament similarly.

It is very interesting to observe in the long history of the Christian church how this particular matter always reappears and receives great prominence at every period of revival and re-awakening. The Protestant Reformers were concerned about it, and the instruction of children in moral and spiritual matters was given great prominence. The Puritans gave it still greater prominence, and the leaders of the Evangelical Awakening of two hundred years ago also did the same. Books have been written about this matter and many sermons preached about it.

This happens, of course, because when people become Christian it affects the whole of their lives. It is not merely something individual and personal; it affects the marriage relationship, and so there are far fewer divorces among

Christian people than among non-Christian people. It also affects the life of the family; it affects the children, it affects the home, it affects every department of human life. The greatest epochs in the history of this country, and of other countries, have always been the years which have followed a religious awakening, a revival of true religion. The moral tone of the whole of society has been raised; even those who have not become Christian have been influenced and affected by it.

In other words, there is no hope of dealing with the moral problems of society except in terms of the gospel of Christ. Right will never be established apart from godliness; but when people become godly they proceed to apply their principles all along the line, and righteousness is seen in the nation at large. But, unfortunately, we have to face the fact that for some reason this aspect of the matter has been sadly neglected in this present century. It is a part of the breakdown that we have been considering in life and morals and the family, the home and other aspects of life. It is a part of the mad rush in which we are all living, and by which we are all influenced so much. For one reason or another the family does not count as it used to do; it is not the centre and the unit that it was formerly. The whole idea of family life has somehow been declining; and this, alas, is partly true in Christian circles also. The family's central importance that is found in the Bible and in all the great periods to which we have referred seems to have disappeared. It is no longer being given the attention and the prominence that it once received. That makes it all the more important for us to discover the principles that should govern us in this respect.

First and foremost, the bringing up of children 'in the nurture and admonition of the Lord' is something which is to be done in the home and by the parents. This is the emphasis throughout the Bible. It is not something that is to be handed over to the school, however good the school may be. It is the duty of parents, their primary and most essential duty. It is their responsibility, and they are not to hand over this responsibility to another. I emphasize this because we are all well aware of what has been happening increasingly during this present century. More and more, parents have been transferring their responsibilities and their duties to the schools.

I regard this as a most serious matter. There is no more important influence in the life of a child than the influence of the home. The home is the fundamental unit of society, and children are born into a home, into a family. There you have the circle that is to be the chief influence in their lives. There is no question about that. It is the biblical teaching everywhere; and it is always in so-called civilizations where ideas concerning the home begin to deteriorate that society ultimately disintegrates.

It thus becomes the business of Christian people to consider and reconsider very carefully the whole question of boarding schools, as to whether it is right to send children to some kind of institutional life, where they spend half of each year or more away from the home and its special peculiar influence. Can that be reconciled with the biblical teaching? The question is urgent because this has become more or less the custom and the practice of virtually all evangelical Christians who can afford to do so.

The teaching of the Scripture is that the child's welfare, the child's soul, should always be the primary consideration; and all matters of prestige, not to use any other term, and all matters of ambition should be put severely aside. Anything that militates against the child's soul, and its knowledge of God and the Lord Jesus Christ, should be rejected. The first consideration invariably should be the soul and its relationship to God. However good the education offered by a boarding school may be, if it militates against the welfare of the soul it must be put on one side. To promote that welfare is the essential element in 'the nurture and admonition of the Lord', and it forms the primary task and duty of the parents.

In the Old Testament it is quite clear that the father was a kind of priest in his household and family; he represented God. He was responsible not only for the morals and the behaviour but for the instruction of his children. The Bible's emphasis everywhere is that this is the primary duty and task of the parents. And it remains so to this day. If we are Christians at all we must realize that this great emphasis is based upon those fundamental units ordained by God: marriage, family, and home. You cannot play fast and loose with them. It is vain to say, as most do about sending children to boarding-schools, 'Everyone is doing this, and it provides a wonderful system of education.' The all-important question is, Is it biblical, is it Christian, is it really ministering to the present and eternal interests of the soul of the child?

I venture the prophecy that the recovery of spirituality and of morals in Great Britain may well come along this line. Christian people will once more have to do their own thinking. We need to be pioneers once more, as God's people in times past have had to be, and the others will then follow. We should be considering to what extent the system of boarding children away from home is responsible for the breakdown of morals in this country. I am not thinking of particular sins only, but of the whole attitude of children towards their own home. A home should not be a place where children spend their holidays. But there are many children to whom home is nothing but a place where they spend their holidays; and their parents, instead of treating them as they should, tend to give them indulgent treatment because they are only home for a while. In that case the whole idea of discipline, and of bringing up the child 'in the nurture and admonition of the Lord', is lost to sight. But, it may be argued, there are many special circumstances. If special circumstances can be proved, I agree. But if there are no special circumstances, the principle I have stated should be the rule; and there are very few special circumstances.

The primary task of the home and of the parents is quite clear. What are parents to do? They are to supplement the teaching of the church, and they are to apply the teaching of the church. So little can be done in a sermon. It has to be applied, to be explained, to be extended, to be supplemented. That is where the parents play their part. And if this has been always right and important, how much more so today than ever before! I ask Christian parents: Have you ever given serious thought to this matter? You face a greater task, perhaps, than parents have ever done, and for the following reason.

Consider what is now being taught the children in the schools. The theory and hypothesis of organic evolution is being taught them as a fact. They are not being presented with it as a mere theory which has not been proved, they are given the impression that it is an absolute fact, and that all people of scientific knowledge and learning believe it. And they are regarded as odd if they do not accept it. We have to meet that situation. Higher-criticism of the Bible is also being taught with its supposed 'assured results'. There are school teachers, to my own knowledge, who are using textbooks which were published thirty or forty years ago. Few of them are aware of the changes that have taken place, even among the 'Higher Critics'.

Children are being taught perverse things in the schools, and they hear them on the radio, and see them on the television. The whole emphasis is anti-God, anti-Bible, anti-true Christianity, anti-miraculous, and anti-supernatural. Who is going to counter these trends? That is precisely the business of parents: 'Bring them up in the nurture and the admonition of the Lord.' It demands great effort by the parents at the present time because the forces against us are so great. Christian parents today have this unusually difficult task of protecting their children against these powerful adverse forces that are trying to indoctrinate them.

There, then, is the setting! To be practical, I wish, in the second place, to show how this is not to be done. There is a way of trying to deal with this situation which is quite disastrous, and does much more harm than good. How is this not to be done? It is never to be done in a mechanical abstract manner, almost 'by numbers', as if it were some sort of drill. I remember an experience of my own in this connection some ten years or so ago. I went to stay with some friends, while I was preaching in a certain place, and I found the wife, the mother of the family, in a state of acute distress. In conversation I discovered the cause of her distress. A certain lady had been there lecturing that very week, her theme being 'How to bring up all the children in your family as good Christians.' It was wonderful! She had five or six children, and she had so organized her home and her life that she finished all her domestic work by nine o'clock in the morning, and then gave herself to various Christian activities. All her children were fine Christians; and it was all so easy, so wonderful. The mother talking to me, who had two children, was in a state of real distress, feeling that she was a complete and utter failure.

What had I to say to her? This: I said, 'Wait a moment; how old are the children of this lady?' I happened to know the answer, and my friend knew also. Not one of them at that time was above the age of sixteen, or thereabouts. I went on: 'Wait and see. This lady tells you that they are all Christians, and that all you need is a scheme which you carry out regularly. Wait a while; the story may be different in a few years.' And, alas, it turned out to be very different. It is doubtful whether more than one of those children is a Christian. Several of them are openly anti-Christian and have turned their backs upon it all. You cannot bring up children to be Christians in that way. It is not a mechanical process, and in any case it was all so cold and clinical. I heard of the same lady giving her same lecture in another place. There, someone was present who had a little understanding and insight. Listening to the address, this other lady made what I thought was a very good comment. She turned to some friends on the way out and said, 'I thank God she was not my mother!' That is laughable, but at the same time there is something tragic about it. What the comment meant was that there was no love there, no warmth. Here was a woman who was proud of herself; she did it all 'by numbers', mechanically. What a wonderful mother she was! This other woman detected that there was no love there, there was no real understanding, there was nothing to warm the heart of a child. A child is not a machine, and so you cannot do this work mechanically.

Nor must the work ever be done in an entirely negative or repressive manner. If you give children the impression that to be religious is to be miserable, and that it consists of prohibitions and constant repression, you may well drive them into the arms of the devil, and into the world. Never be entirely negative and repressive. I meet tragedies constantly in this respect. People talk to me at the end of a service and they say, 'This is the first time I have been in a chapel for twenty years or so.' I ask, 'How is that?' Then they tell me that they had reacted against the harshness and the repressive character of the religion in which they were brought up. They had no conception of Christianity at all. What they saw was not Christianity, but a harsh man-made religion, a false Puritanism. There are still people, alas!, who only present a caricature of true Puritanism, and have never understood its real teaching. They have seen the negative but have never seen the positive. That does great harm.

Thirdly, in bringing up our children in 'the nurture and admonition of the Lord', we must never do so in such a way as to make little prigs and hypocrites of them. I have seen much of that also. To me it is very sad, and indeed revolting, to hear children using pious phrases which they do not understand. But their parents are proud of them and say, 'Listen to them, isn't it wonderful?' The children are too young to understand such things. I know that many children like to play at preaching. Such childish behaviour may be excusable, but when you get the parents thinking that it is wonderful, and putting up the children to do it before the admiring gaze of adults, then it is almost blasphemy. It is certainly very harmful to the child. It is to turn them into little prigs, to make little hypocrites of them.

My last negative at this point is that we must never force a child to a decision. What trouble and havoc has been wrought by this! 'Isn't it marvellous?', say the parents. 'My little So-and-So, a mere youngster, decided for Christ.' Pressure had been brought to bear in the meeting. But that should never be done; you are violating the personality of the child. In addition, of course, you are displaying a profound ignorance of the way of salvation. You can make a little child decide anything. You have the power and the ability to do so; but it is wrong, it is unchristian, it is not spiritual.

In other words we must never be too direct in this matter, especially with a child, never be too emotional. If your child feels uncomfortable as you are talking to him about spiritual matters, or if you are talking to someone else's child and he feels uncomfortable, your method is obviously wrong. The child should never be made to feel uncomfortable. If he does it is because you are too direct, or you are too emotional, or you are bringing pressure to bear. That is not the way to do this work.

I have known some real tragedies in this respect also. I recollect the case of two young men in particular before they reached the age of fifteen or sixteen. Their parents were always pushing them forward. In the one case, one of the parents used to write about her children and give the impression that they were outstanding Christians. Both these young men have repudiated the Christian faith utterly and entirely by today, and have no use for it. Christian parents must always remember that they are handling a life, a personality, a soul. My counsel is: Do not bring pressure to bear upon your children. Do not force them to a decision. I know the anxiety felt by a parent. It is very natural; but if we are spiritual, if we are 'filled with the Spirit', we shall never violate a personality, never bring any unfair pressure to bear upon a child. So our teaching must never be too direct, or too emotional. It must never be done in such a manner that the children are made to feel disloyal to us if they do not profess belief. That is unforgivable.

What, then, is the true way? Let me give some suggestions. There used to be at one time in people's houses, and I still see them sometimes, a little card hanging on the wall with this sentence on it, 'Christ is the Head of this house.' I am not an advocate of putting up such cards or texts; but there was something good in the idea. In the Old Testament we read that instructions were given to the children of Israel to 'Write them (the words of the Lord) on the door-posts', the reason being that we are such forgetful creatures. The early Protestants used to paint the Ten Commandments on the walls of their churches partly for the same reason. But whether you do, or do not, display a card, the important point is that the impression should always be given that Christ is the Head of the house or the home.

How is that impression given? Chiefly by your general conduct and example! The parents should be living in such a way that the children should always have a feeling that they themselves are under Christ, that Christ is their Head. The fact should be obvious in their conduct and behaviour. Above all, there should be an atmosphere of love.

'Be not drunk with wine, wherein is excess; but be filled with the Spirit.' That is our controlling text in this as in all these particular applications. The fruit of the Spirit is love, and if the home is filled with an atmosphere of the love produced by the Spirit, most of its problems are solved. That is what does the work, not the direct pressures and appeals, but an atmosphere of love.

What else? General conversation! At the table or wherever you are, general conversation is most important. We listen perhaps to the news on the radio, and conversation begins about the news. Great affairs are being mentioned, international affairs, politics, industrial troubles, etc. A part of our task in bringing up our children in the nurture and admonition of the Lord is to see to it that even such general conversation is always conducted in Christian terms. We should always bring in the Christian point of view. The children will hear other people talking about the same things. They may be walking along the road, and they hear two men arguing about the very things that they had heard discussed at home. At once they will notice one big difference; the whole approach was different at home.

In other words the Christian point of view must be brought into the whole of life. Whether you are discussing international affairs or local affairs, personal matters or business matters – whatever it is, everything must be considered under this general heading of Christianity. This is a most vital point, for when this is done, the children unconsciously become aware of the fact that there is a governing principle in the lives of their parents; their thinking and everything else about them is different from all that they see and hear in the unbelieving world. The whole atmosphere is different. Thus the children, gradually and partly unconsciously, become aware that there is such a thing as a Christian point of view. That is a real achievement. Once they get hold of that fact the problem becomes much easier.

The next matter is the answering of questions. There the Christian parent gets a great opportunity. It is sometimes extremely difficult, I know; but we are given the opportunity of answering questions. I like the way in which the matter is introduced in the sixth chapter of Deuteronomy, in the twentieth verse: 'And when thy son asketh thee in time to come, saying, What mean the testimonies, and the statutes, and the judgments, which the LORD our God hath commanded you? Then thou shalt say unto thy son, We were Pharaoh's bondmen in Egypt: and the Lord brought us out of Egypt with a mighty hand', and so on. In other words, a day will come when the children will ask a question such as this: 'Why don't you do this or that? The father and mother of my little friend do this, why don't you?' There you have been given an opportunity of bringing up your child 'in the nurture and admonition of the Lord'. But if we are to take it, we must know the right answer, and be able to supply it. You cannot 'give a reason for the hope that is in you', you cannot bring up your children in the nurture and admonition of the Lord, unless you know your Bible and its teaching. 'Why don't you do this, why don't you do that? My friends' fathers spend their evenings in public houses; you don't. They spend their evenings in clubs, they spend their nights dancing; you don't. Why? What is the difference?'

When questioned in that way you must not brush the child aside and say, 'Well, we are all different, you see, and this is how we prefer it.' No, you say rather to your child: 'We are all alike at heart to begin with; and we behave in this different way not because we are naturally better than others. That is not the explanation. It is not that I have one temperament and the other fathers have other temperaments. We are all "born in sin", we are all slaves by nature to various things. There is something wrong within us all, there is an evil principle in us all and none of us knows God truly. You see, the difference is this, that God has caused me to see how wrong certain things are. But I would still be like your friends' fathers, were it not that I believe and know that God sent his only Son, the Lord Jesus of whom you have heard, into the world to rescue us, to deliver us.'

Thus you introduce the gospel; you have to decide how much to give. It depends upon the age of the child. But answer his questions, let him know, let him know exactly, when he asks his question, why you live as you do. You must not foist it on him, you must not preach at him; but if he asks his question, then tell him, tell him very simply. Tell him more and more as he gets older; but always be ready to answer the questions. Know your facts, understand your gospel, build yourself up in it, so that you can impart it and pass it on. Thus you will be able to bring up your children in 'the nurture and admonition of the Lord'.

Then you can guide their reading. Get them to read good biographies. Biographies will appeal to them. Guide their reading in various ways; turn their minds in the right direction, and familiarize them with the glories of the Christian faith in action.

What else? Be careful always, whenever you have a meal, to return thanks to God for it, and to ask his blessing upon it. This is rarely done today by any except those who are Christians. If your children become accustomed to hearing you thanking God, and returning thanks, and asking a blessing, it will do something for them. Go further. Have what is called a family altar, which means that once, at least, every day you should meet together as a family round the Word of God. The father as the head of the house should read a portion of Scripture and offer a simple prayer. It need not be long, but let him acknowledge God and let him thank God for the Lord Jesus Christ. Let the children hear the Word of God regularly. If they ask questions about it, answer them. Give them instruction as you are able to do so. Be wise, be judicious. Do not make of it something distasteful, hateful, or boring; make it such that they will look forward to it, something they will like and in which they find delight.

In other words, to sum it all up: what we have to do is to make Christianity attractive. We should give our children the impression that the most wonderful thing in the world is Christianity; and that there is nothing in life comparable to being a Christian. We should create within them the desire to be like us. They see us and they see the joy that we have in it, and the way we marvel and wonder at it all. They should be saying to themselves, I am longing to be as old as they are, so that I can enjoy it as they obviously do. Our method must never be mechanical, legal, repressive. Our testimony must never be forced, but in all we are and do and say, let them know that we ourselves are 'bond-slaves of Jesus Christ', that God in his grace has opened our eyes and awakened us to the most glorious thing in the world, and that our greatest desire for them is that they may enter into the same knowledge and have the same joy, and have the highest privilege possible in this world, that of serving the Lord and living to the praise of the glory of his grace.

Whatever your work, whether business or profession or manual labour or preaching, do all things to the glory of God, and in that way you will bring up your children 'in the nurture and the admonition of the Lord'.

ALSO BY DR MARTYN LLOYD-JONES FROM EPHESIANS CHAPTER 5

Christian Marriage

from basic principles to transformed relationships

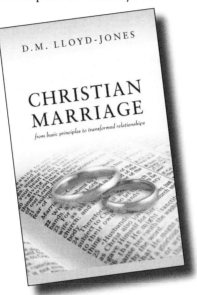

In an age which has seen an almost total collapse of marriage and when, in many cases, marriages end in divorce with children being raised in 'broken homes', Dr Lloyd-Jones' words speak powerfully into our present situation. It is a situation which may be seen as giving Christians, and especially Christian marriages, a valuable opportunity to bear witness to biblical truth. The way in which Dr Lloyd-Jones, like the Apostle Paul, deals with the marriage relationship, is extremely important - to attempt to deal with Christian practice apart from Christian doctrine is to tread a dangerous path. As these chapters on Ephesians make clear, the only Christianity powerful enough to penetrate and change society is that which is derived from the work of the Spirit of God.

ISBN 978 1 84871 124 2, 200 pp., paperback

THE BANNER OF TRUTH

The Banner of Truth Trust originated in 1957 in London. The founders believed that much of the best literature of historic Christianity had been allowed to fall into oblivion and that, under God, its recovery could well lead not only to a strengthening of the church today but to true revival.

Inter-denominational in vision, this publishing work is now international, and our lists include a number of contemporary authors along with classics from the past. The translation of these books into many languages is encouraged.

A monthly magazine, *The Banner of Truth*, is also published and further information will be gladly supplied by either of the offices below.

THE BANNER OF TRUTH TRUST

3 Murrayfield Road PO Box 621, Carlisle
Edinburgh, EH12   Pennsylvania, 17013
6EL   USA

www.banneroftruth.co.uk